Finding Einstein: My IEP Journey

Finding Einstein

My IEP Journey

Based on the Blog, *LA Mediocre Mommy*

Lia Martin

LOS ANGELES, CALIFORINIA

www.myiepjourney.com

ISBN: 978-0-9981931-2-0

Printed in the United States of America

Library of Congress Control Number: 2016921250
Northland Publishing Company, Cleveland, OHIO

The content in this book is not intended to be a substitute for professional medical advice, diagnosis, or treatment. Always seek the advice of a physician or other qualified
health provider with any questions you may have regarding your child's condition.

*For my family and other families who have
children who learn differently.*

"I learn from my failures."
–Tay, age 8

IDEA is a federal law that requires school districts to provide a "free appropriate public education" (FAPE) to eligible children with disabilities. A free appropriate public education means that special education and related services are to be provided as described in an individualized education program (IEP) and under public supervision to your child at no cost to you. An IEP is the written plan that describes a child's abilities and needs and the placement and services designed to meet the child's unique needs. A student must have an IEP before he or she receives special education services. A student's IEP must be implemented as soon as possible after the IEP meeting. In addition, a student's IEP must be reviewed and, if necessary, revised once a year or more often upon request.

Table of Contents

Prologue

I have a recurring dream that places me on the second floor of an indigo blue two-story Victorian home, architecturally akin to the one in which I reside. Well, okay—if you must know, there are a few minor differences. I actually live in a yellow ranch-style home, and in my dream, my tile floors have transformed into Berber carpet.

I am standing outside on a window ledge. My loose stomach flops in the sluggish wind while I tremble and search for something to grab for stability. I find myself here though among my litany of neuroses is a fear of heights.

Just as I must decide whether or not to jump to the concrete driveway, I awake. I'm drenched in perspiration—most likely from perimenopause. Then I hear the voice of my husband or one of my two children, and calm arrives. I am no longer the frightened woman of my dream. I have shifted to Mom. I am a mother, wife, and advocate who occasionally tells jokes on stage (primarily about being a mother, wife, and advocate).

Since I've started the mom profession, I've found myself frequently updating the job description. I signed up for perfectly behaved children who responded to the techniques I'd read about in all of the psychology books and articles, back when I was a college journalism student. Obviously, preposterous thinking played an equal role in my early parenting ideals.

Life, however, is much more layered.

My son Tay, has ADHD and is also a gifted artist. He doesn't appear to be any different than a typical student. But he finds it challenging to decode social cues, appropriately express his emotions, and keep track of all of the thoughts that roam around his head at any given moment. So this mom has been through countless school meetings with psychologists, specialists, and a plethora of school staff over how to shepherd my son successfully through elementary school. And despite my naïve optimism, we chalked up many failed attempts before we finally got it right. Once, I even allowed a numerologist to provide an assessment over the phone. You know what they say about desperate times.

My experience with kids early in life should have groomed me. I've always loved children. Like many people, I counted on babysitting for my primary source of income from junior high through late high school. My childcare résumé included a young lady with Down syndrome, a boy suspected of having ADHD, and my charge as a volunteer camp counselor for the Muscular Dystrophy Association. Yet nothing I did before I became a mother quite prepared me for my journey with son, who is twice exceptional (gifted with a learning disability) son.

Before Tay came along, I ranked among those judgmental people without kids. I'd stare at the uncontrollable two-year-old in the department store whose exasperated mother looked as though she hadn't taken a shower in days, and I'd still think, "How hard could it be?"

But as it turns out, watching someone's child for a few hours does not compare to the day-to-day work of raising one.

I learned this quickly once Tay was born. I became the one who hadn't taken a shower and who faced down my audience of stares as I dragged my son screaming out of the neighborhood Target. Unbeknownst to me at the time, Tay had more than just tantrums; he had specific triggers that caused his outbursts. On that list of triggers: the overstimulation of a crowded, brightly lit store. They hadn't covered that in any of those parenting articles I read.

To this day, I still feel woefully inept at providing Tay the full support he needs. And because I've told jokes about my feelings of incompetence on stage and posted about it on Twitter and Facebook, I know there are other parents out there who feel like me. Since you're reading my book, you might be one of them. Or perhaps you are a parent sympathizer.

Whatever the case, I'm glad you're on this journey. You are in the company of remarkable people with imaginative ideas about how our kids learn. And I'm happy to tell you many groundbreaking organizations and advances have sprung up recently to address the needs of children with learning disabilities (more affectionately referred to as learning differences)—kids like ours.

If you have the kind of kid who hasn't entered the classroom seamlessly, and now you're having doubts about that Harvard acceptance letter you once envisioned—or you're wondering how you'll even survive the next school year—this book is for you. I wrote this guide to let you know you're not alone.

Contrary to how it may seem to others (or more likely, to yourself), you are not a bad parent. You're not even a mediocre parent. You are the parent of a unique child. And there are tools and techniques that may help your child, despite his or her challenges in school.

In the pages of this publication, I share some hard-earned insights about one of my son's particular struggles--ADHD. But more importantly, I provide an honest, intimate account of my struggles to get my son a game-changing individualized education program (IEP). It's my sincere hope that in these pages, you'll be able to gather the information you need to feel well equipped to advocate for your child or support any parent who needs it.

If you feel like you're standing on a window ledge without a safety net to catch you if you make a misstep, I'm there with you. While I don't have all of the answers, I'm willing to give you what I do have: resources, encouragement, and a few laughs along the way.

Those Germs

Lyrics by Tay at three years-old

Kids across the land
You gotta understand
When you play outside
You gotta clean your hands
It's good to really scrub
To get off all the grub
'Cause if you forget
You might get really sick
Those germs can get you
sick, sick, sick
Yeah, those germs can get you
get you, get you
It's fun to play outside
It's fun to ride your bike
But listen across the land
You better wash those hands
Those germs can get you
sick, sick, sick
Yeah, those germs, can get you
get you
They get you sick, sick, sick
Yeah, those germs can get you
get you, get you

One of Those Days

Wednesday morning. The scent of verbena flowers and Bermuda grass seeped through the splintered window screens of my San Fernando Valley home. Unlike most mornings, when I claw through my children's cluttered clothing drawers to form outfits that may or may not coordinate, on that day my husband had already stacked and separated their gear.

In theory, my son Tay's required uniform made his ensemble a tad easy. He had two colors to choose from: navy blue and white. But the varied combination choices of those two colors occasionally birthed a wardrobe standoff between us. Some mornings he wanted to wear a turtleneck, despite the weather forecast of ninety-plus degrees. Other days, he wanted his frayed jeans because they made him feel cool. The beloved transformer gloves he liked to keep hidden in his backpack for "later" (probably for a puppet show during language arts) also caused conflict. Occasionally, tags scratched, material itched, or panic arose because we were behind schedule.

That Wednesday morning stood out from the rest because of the comfort I felt when I realized my husband had acquired a great deal of insight. After fourteen years of marriage and eight years of parenting together, something clicked. He was well versed on the parts of my daily routine that heightened my early morning anxiety: the dissipating box of yerba mate tea, the frustrating effort to remember where I last hid my cell phone from our kids, the struggle to get our little ones dressed ten minutes before jetting from the house for school.

My four-year-old daughter and eight-year-old son were also accustomed to my morning mania, which ceremonially ended with a prayer in the car for a day of peace and patience. During that spiritual automobile gathering, Tay frequently interjected with his own version of how the day might go.

Tay wanted a spaceship to land on the lawn of his school, or a volcano to erupt in the middle of the street. In other words, he always wanted something extraordinary to happen. He even drew some of his fantastical fables or sang them in the songs he crafted. My daughter laughed from the pit of her protruding belly at his stories. Tay had a huge fan in his sister.

Those were the easy moments parenting a child with a learning difference. I wanted to savor them like a perfectly buttered waffle with my favorite brand of Grade A organic, maple syrup.

But those moments didn't last. They couldn't. My son's behavior frequently shifted unpredictably. And that's what happened on that Wednesday morning.

By the time we arrived in front of the chaotic drop-off spot at his elementary school, Tay's chockfull-of-agitation energy set in. As soon as he removed his seatbelt, he began searching. Something was missing. His lunch.

At first I didn't think much of it, as he'd much rather play, draw, or compose songs in his head during meals than eat anyway. While Tay hadn't been officially diagnosed, but I suspected he had sensory processing disorder (SPD). Children with SPD sometimes overreact or underreact to touch, sounds, and food textures. Though some doctors don't acknowledge it as a disorder, in my experience, it is plenty real for parents. If a food has a strong smell for Tay, he won't consume it. And if other people around him are eating something that bothers his senses, he'll move to another room or refrain from eating altogether.

Despite his lukewarm relationship with food, Tay's angst over the missing lunch grew. I later realized the one thing that eluded me—routine—was essential to Tay. The slightest change in the day's predictability could transition to chaos. Tay didn't even like for me to take alternate routes to school. He needed to know the destination and the course.

Tay always brought lunch to school and it always contained the same items: a peanut-free granola bar, organic gummies, an organic vanilla protein shake, and SunChips he had to crush before consumption. So the morning we left it behind, tears and aggravation ensued. I assured him I'd get a meal to him by lunchtime.

"Okay," he said, then walked off toward the school. In my mind, crisis over. Problem solved.

As usual, I scanned through my work email on my smartphone before setting out to drop off Kid Number Two. My daughter waved goodbye to Tay, then sang along with Katy Perry's "Roar" on the radio.

Unbeknownst to me, while Radio Disney blasted, Tay threw himself into the school's maidenhair ferns at the school entrance in despair over his missing lunch. He quickly garnered the attention of another parent, who tried to coax him out to no avail. His behavior escalated into a full-blown tantrum. I heard none of this.

As I turned the ignition, the school principal walked up and motioned for me to roll down the window. She asked about the scene that I'd completely missed. I looked over by the door of the school where three or four people stood talking. The principal had rounded up Tay's aide and a couple of staff to assist with handling him, all while I was engrossed in my "day job." They stood gathered for a post-tantrum analysis and the principal gave me the rundown.

I would've been mortified had we been anywhere else. But that was our third elementary school—and the most tolerant climate we'd experienced to date. It was home.

The principal spoke evenly. "Tay had a bit of an episode, but he's off to class now." She assured me everything was fine, but asked, "So, you are going to come back with lunch? Seems like it's a pretty big deal to him." She smiled. And I drove to a nearby store to pick up food as quickly as legally possible.

I believe Tay's tantrum got de-escalated so quickly that day because he had an individualized education program (IEP) in place. Both the principal and her staff already knew Tay had meltdowns from time to time, and they'd worked out ways to calm him down. By the time that meltdown happened, everyone was prepared and Tay felt safe.

Our IEP is the culmination of many long (and sometimes boring) meetings and stacks of paperwork. In those meetings, among other things, we strategized about how to handle my son specifically at times like the one I've just described. When we began, I didn't have much information about what an IEP would mean. I was just a mom trying to figure out how to make school less torturous for my child. Now, friends and family faced with similar challenges ask for my insight.

The road to finding a good school environment for my son was circuitous, to say the least. This is because our IEP journey began in preschool. But at the time, I had no idea.

Chapter 2

When There's No Napping at Naptime

My upbringing played a large role in my approach to parenting. I spent most of my childhood in a small suburb of Cleveland, Ohio. It might as well have been the Deep South. As far as parenting is concerned, Ohio is a different world from the one occupied by the granola-eating, Birkenstock-wearing, protest-marching moms and dads I've observed on the West Coast, where I'm raising my children today.

During most of her career, my mother taught second grade, so she got home from work at a reasonable hour. As a divorcée who raised me and my brother primarily on her own, she relied heavily on neighbors and friends for support. Single-parent families rarely existed in suburban neighborhoods back then, so there were no roadmaps for my mother to follow. She largely relied on her gut. In a life absent of talk shows, Twitter feeds, and blogs to guide her through single motherhood, she drew on pure instinct and visceral guesswork. Sometimes it worked. When it didn't, she sent us to Grandma's.

In elementary school, our mother required us to go to the neighborhood babysitter, Mrs. Maggie after school. We had to wait in Mrs. Maggie's linoleum-tiled basement, where she watched us until our mom arrived. We loved our sitter. She wore oversized, brightly colored cotton housedresses, a short, curly, salt-and-pepper afro, and ragged slippers. She smoked incessantly; I think her cigarettes of choice were Marlboro Red 100's. She had a beautiful, raspy singing voice and would belt out Dolly Parton tunes on command.

Mrs. Maggie also fed us massive pancakes drenched in faux maple syrup at snack time and allowed us to watch all of the cartoons our eyes could take (heaven, for us). On the other hand, if children acted "bad," Mrs. Maggie retrieved her long, thin, leather belt and went to town on their behinds. Her older children did the same.

I escaped Mrs. Maggie's wrath because of my status as the quiet kid who went virtually unnoticed much of my youth. As a low-maintenance child, I sat in corners drawing or writing poetry and even found myself left behind on school field trips. I was that inconspicuous.

Not the case for my precocious brother. Due to his abundance of energy and the unlimited ways he dismantled practically every appliance he came into contact with, he received spankings regularly. These were distributed without regard to what motivated his behavior. Back then, spank first, ask questions … never.

Corporal punishment also got meted out in our local public school. By junior high, I'd figured out a clever way around it. I realized the principal sent students back to class with a pass that confirmed they'd received a swat. I stole a stack of those passes, forged the principal's signature, and each time a teacher sent me out of class for my swat, I played in the bathroom for a while. Then I returned with my most exasperated fake post-swat face and sheepishly gave my illegal pass to my teacher. I also sold the swat passes to friends. The most egregious offense I committed as a child happens to be one of my proudest.

I wasn't a bad student. Just a quiet student with a stash of contraband hall passes. But because of my endless daydreaming and doodling, I wasn't a model student either. I drew everything from flowers to clothing during almost every class. I sketched on the corners of notebooks and inside of book covers and even, God forbid, on the actual pages of the books! What's more, I carried forbidden candy in my pockets. Without those passes, a large measure of paddle swats would definitely have become one of my indelible school memories.

If kids repeatedly exhibited unacceptable behavior at our suburban school, those children were simply labeled "bad kids." Many boys, like my brother, met this fate. People believed that despite their behavior, they were "fine"; however, that wasn't always the case. Some of those "bad" boys from my childhood disengaged from school and ended up dropping out altogether. Others were placed in remedial courses (or even in an entire separate part of the school building) where they didn't receive the opportunity to build skills necessary to succeed later in life.

When I was in college, I received a call from one of these mislabeled boys. The call came from a prison, and I chose not to take it. In hindsight, I've often wondered about boys like the one who ended up incarcerated. Were those "bad" classmates just good kids who had learning disabilities no one caught? Might things have turned out better for them had they been taught the academic and social skills necessary to be successful, if someone had just believed in them? Those experiences shaped me and planted the seed for my parenting style. Years before the birth of my son, I decided I'd never let any child of mine be labeled "bad"; I'd protect him from such a vacuous diagnosis. I had no idea just how vigorously I'd have to confront this issue head on.

***

Tay's school experience was completely different from mine. His experience in preschool trumps my entire school career, including college (where my first real heartbreak occurred).

Tay attended a home-based preschool first. A nice, clean, home without any particularly remarkable interior or exterior décor, and recommended by a friend, it seemed safe. When I first met the firm but loving director—let's call her Ms. Sally—I felt comfortable leaving Tay in her hands.

But Tay didn't last long there. Though Ms. Sally knew about Tay's peanut allergy, he got hold of some while he was in her care. He had a severe reaction, breaking out in a rash, and she gave him Benadryl. Luckily, that did the trick. But I realized Ms. Sally and I had dissimilar philosophies on discipline. She thought it best to yell at the young children when they did something wrong or dangerous, instead of encouraging them to change course.

For example, some instructors guide behavior with humor. One time, Tay decided to belly flop into a kiddie pool. His teacher at the time simply shook her head, smiled, and asked him if that felt good. He never did it again. Others may give a child two correct choices, so that he or she feels empowered. There are many ways to get a child to behave appropriately, and I have yet to read anything that suggests yelling is one of them.

After preschool number one came the allegedly progressive school between my job and our home. Before long, the non-credentialed teaching assistant, who had no experience working with active children, found herself frequently exasperated with Tay. It became clear that his level of activity fell outside of the norm. Unfortunately, the inexperienced teacher's aide unwittingly escalated matters. She referred to Tay as "defiant" and "a behavior problem." (I waited for the word "thug" but she never used it.) Without a medical degree of any sort, she suggested he had a chemical imbalance. Because we'd adopted Tay, she suggested he might have suffered from pre-natal drug exposure. That was not the case. I had experienced my introduction to what I now know is teacher bias. This is when a teacher's background and experience causes him or her to make assumptions about a student which are often negative.

Tay's behavior took a turn for the worse. He had fights with classmates and uncontrollable tantrums. When he transitioned from one activity to the next, he melted down. Though Tay was protective of younger children, his aggressiveness toward classmates resulted in many notes and phone calls to me weeks later.

Then after a heart-racing incident in which a teacher delayed administering Tay's EpiPen because she was fearful and reluctant, I pulled him out of preschool number two. Another toddler had given him candy with peanuts at the purportedly peanut-free establishment, and Tay had gone into anaphylactic shock. I worked downtown, but with Los Angeles traffic I might as well have been in Siberia. The drive time severely impaired my ability to get him his medicine quickly. For five tormenting minutes, I had to convince the teacher over the phone to save my kid's life. She finally gave him the medicine, which restored his breathing to normal. I had finally had enough.

After that fearful incident at the progressive school, I enrolled Tay in the Montessori school where, I later found out, television shows passed for curriculum. I'm not sure how that aligned with Maria Montessori's original vision of education, but Tay regularly came home quoting lines from popular cartoons. Meanwhile, that Disney Channel education took almost my entire paycheck. I decided I needed to pull Tay out of preschool number three before he memorized all of the dialogue from *Shrek*.

At the time, to comfort me, many of my male friends assured me they'd had exhibited behavior similar to Tay's when they were children: running into walls, jumping off furniture, even violent tantrums when things didn't go their way.

But I sensed Tay's struggles might be different than what my friends said they went through. I couldn't identify how at the time, but Tay's activity level and emotional outbursts seemed out of the ordinary. I had no idea why. I started to worry that his future would include a "bad kid" label, like some of the classmates from my youth. I knew how that turned out for some of them, and this prospect frightened me. So I stayed up nights conducting Internet research, and I visited preschool locations from one end of the San Fernando Valley to the other. I became exhausted by my efforts to find the right fit for Tay.

As it turned out, his challenging behavior in preschool was not about his conduct. Instead, it was a clue—or many clues—to his learning difference. He didn't have the language yet to express himself. He used the only thing he knew how to: his body. That meant running when it was too loud in the classroom, pushing a classmate when their smell was too pungent for Tay, or hitting himself as way to calm his body. Sadly, no one recognized those signs. Not even me.

I knew he needed a new preschool. I focused on searching for a place like the school I remembered fondly from my childhood. I wanted a safe environment where he could be nurtured. But as I was learning, that's not as easy to accomplish as it should be.

Then, as I faced a whole new challenge, Tay's struggles temporarily faded to the background.

Chapter 3

What Doesn't Kill Us

Some years ago, my mother and I and decided to spend our Mothers' Days at a spa together. Previously, I'd celebrated that holiday with my in-laws. Having successfully planned several fundraisers, a few birthday parties, and four weddings, including my own, I became the family event planner. So on Mother's Day, I always picked the restaurant. If my mother-in-law approved, that's where we ate.

Due to Tay's behavior, I had to secure family-friendly establishments. One Mother's Day, approximately six years ago, I found the perfect place (according to Yelp). I also had some big news to share with my loved ones.

When my husband, Tay, and I arrived, my in-laws were already seated and prepared to order. Before the waitress could ask what we wanted, I placed an ultrasound photo on the table.

My father-in-law asked, "What is that?" and my mother-in-law asked, "Who does that belong to?" The ultrasound introduced our peanut-sized daughter, conceived sometime after my forty-second birthday.

No one was more excited than Tay that morning, as he relived the joy of hearing about his imminent playmate. He'd known about the baby as soon as the doctor said we were clear to share. The baby's first weeks in vitro had been uncertain; she'd been slow to develop a heartbeat and fetal pole. But once clearance came and we told Tay, fun sibling stories abounded. He was thrilled by every opportunity he had to tell his own anticipatory version.

Tay could be very protective of small children. Anytime a baby hit him or pushed him, he'd laugh and gently tell the infant "no." In church, in lieu of attending Sunday School class with students his age, Tay sometimes sat with me while I watched the infants in the daycare room. He sang to them or made them giggle—easier for him than staying put through lessons.

As weeks wore on, we discussed with Tay the arrival of our daughter. He loved her before birth, but he hoped she was really a he. We decided to impress upon him the importance of being a big brother, regardless of his sibling's gender. I included Tay in my baby preparation, taking him shopping for her clothes and furniture. They'd have to share a room since our home was small. That didn't bother Tay, who'd already carved out the perfect sibling space in his bedroom.

Tay became more excited. I became more fatigued.

***

Shortly after I announced my pregnancy, my grandmother passed away. She'd been my last living grandparent, and I experienced a bittersweet trip home. I had affectionate memories from when, during her tenure as my elementary school principal, she walked me to school. A pastor's daughter, she'd ironically given me my first lecture on "the Pill." Because of the special bond we shared, it grieved me that she wouldn't meet her great-granddaughter. Speaking at her funeral service gave me some comfort. Through her profession as an educator, she'd touched many lives.

Soon after my grandmother's death, my husband, sister-in-law, and I found ourselves in the midst of an unforeseen family crisis. In the backyard of my husband's childhood suburban home, my father-in-law told us his doctors had discovered "a spot" on his lungs. Stunned, my husband asked questions about what "a spot" meant. But details never surfaced. A traditionalist, the family patriarch did not make a habit of sharing intimate aspects of his life. I believe he wanted to protect us, as his children. He wanted us to go on with our lives and allow him his with laughter and positive memories.

The back-to-back family blows took a toll on me. One weekend afternoon, I stood at the gas stove in my mint-green kitchen and attempted to prepare lunch. Instead, I called my aunt, sobbing uncontrollably. As the reasonable one in the family, she seemed like the logical choice to discuss my feelings with. She told me to let go of things I couldn't control, that my emotional outbursts couldn't help me or the baby. So I took a moment, straightened up, and finished making lunch. I worked on the difficult task of keeping my emotions on a tight leash over the subsequent several weeks. Eventually, the difficult became the norm.

I spent most of my evenings alone. My husband spent his evenings visiting with his father or attending events with his friends. While Tay slept, I researched possible future charter and magnet elementary schools with mission statements that contained wording like "inclusion" or "creative teaching."

During that time of upheaval in my family life, my work life shifted as well. My workday included rumors about personnel adjustments at all levels. The head of human resources offered me a management position (I supported the chief operating officer as her executive assistant). But coworkers suggested I turn the promotion down. Instead, people suggested I leave the organization (as a few of them did). Eventually, the COO was laid off, and the entire dynamic of the organization transformed from a focus on our mission to scrutiny over how long people took on their breaks or lunches or whether employees chatted too much. My coworkers began to labor under a sense of paranoia and panic.

The uncertainty at work compounded a tenuous grip I'd started to feel on my marriage, as well as the incompetence I'd begun to feel as a mother. As customary, I pretended. I made jokes. I coped. I concentrated on planning my escape from the job and allowing my husband to be with his father as much as possible. That meant solo trips to all of my pre-natal doctor's visits and hospital tours. And so began the phase of isolation I felt in our marriage. I transitioned from a participant in to a spectator of our relationship.

Tay frequently accompanied his father to visit Grandpa at the Kaiser Hospital, and I met my husband and son there a few times. Though Tay knew little about his grandfather's illness, he decided to take his pretend doctor's kit to all hospital visits. When Tay walked in with his plastic medical bag, the doctors and nurses praised him, even asking about Tay's future plans in the medical field.

I smiled while I secretly panicked over successfully navigating him through preschool. I had few thoughts beyond that. I wanted to get that right for Tay. I wanted to succeed at his education because I believed that if I could get it right, it would be the one thing going well at the time. The one thing I could control. Or so I thought.

I used the time I spent alone to hone in on Tay's education. I made the choice to allow my husband and me to live separate lives. It felt more manageable than trying to awaken the dead.

Pregnant, spent, and worried about my job, the baby in my belly, and my son, I took an emotional reprieve from my post as wife. But walking that road would have consequences later.

Chapter 4

A Place Where He Belongs

In spite of my pregnant belly, I landed a new gig. I couldn't believe it. They hired me with the understanding that I'd be dropping my load (baby) just months after my hire date. I never mentioned that I'd spent a few days on stress-related bedrest while at my previous job. I had faith that sort of issue would not recur in the future.

A big perk: unlike my last position, the new one put me back in the entertainment industry. I'd still be working in an administrative capacity, but being around other creatives would be inspiring.

The camaraderie and energy at my new job was a welcome change from the turmoil at my former organization. Decorations and toys adorned my desk frequently. Afternoons, we gathered around in a circle for songs; holidays turned into decorating contests; birthdays looked like full-on film sets. Writers found each other and exchanged scripts during down time. TV monitors and music played through headsets. No one cared how long coworkers took lunch, as long as work got done. A general feeling of happiness filled the playful space.

Soon after starting work, I officially informed Tay's preschool director of my decision to place him elsewhere. For some reason, I didn't want to hurt her feelings, so I explained that I wanted to have both my children at the same location. His current school started at two years old, while many others in the area started as early as six weeks.

After visiting a slew of locations, I pinpointed Tay's fourth preschool. It fell under the supervision of the school district near my new office. I'd taken a pay cut at the new job, partly to be closer to our home, and now, I'd pay even more tuition than I had previously. So preschool number four had one certain drawback: it totally annihilated my shoe budget.

But my intuition told me this preschool would work out for Tay. As a school district center, the preschool's requirements aligned with those of the local elementary schools. And all of the area schools performed well. The preschool also had space for the baby; I made sure she was on the waiting list before birth.

Tay's new primary instructor was a woman in her sixties with a soft voice and a comforting disposition. She was barely over five feet tall, round, and reminiscent of the Old Lady in the Shoe drawings in one of my favorite childhood books.

Tay's challenging behavior continued with her, but rather than punish him for his transgressions, she did the opposite. She hugged him. Some days, during naptime, she embraced him the entire time other children slept in their blue daycare cots, comforted by their animated-character blankets from home. He needed the human touch. He craved it. Tay was always affectionate and liked to sit on the laps of close relatives. That level of affection just didn't take place in preschool—until we found that one. Naptime had become especially difficult as Tay simply couldn't wind himself down after the stimulation from whatever he learned that morning. But it didn't matter to his new teacher. She was in the trenches with him, helping him to cope via something basically human—love.

As Tay's teacher became comfortable with me, she became more assertive about strategies to help him, which included dietary advice. She wrote me notes about what she preferred to see in his lunch box. She'd seen patterns in his behavior that seemed to relate to certain foods, such as an inability to sleep and aggressiveness. The new list of acceptable foods included snap peas, applesauce, yogurt, and chicken nuggets.

His teacher also rewarded appropriate choices with affirmations and coveted stickers. She found opportunities to praise his appropriate actions and ignored inappropriate ones. It seemed that everyone was good at pointing out Tay's mistakes, but none of us were proficient at acknowledging his accomplishments. We especially failed at recognizing small victories, such as sitting through a meal, or until the end of a book at story time. This instructor's arsenal included tools completely foreign to me, but they proved to have encouraging effects. I came to understand that her method had an actual name: positive reinforcement.

Phone calls about tantrums slowed significantly. Giggles chimed out at our parent-teacher meeting. Though Tay still had tough days, I saw a much happier boy.

At the end of the school year, Tay attended his preschool graduation with a broad smile and professed his fervent passion for spaceships. Proud of his freshly cut red curly locks, he ran in his "big boy" formal slacks to meet friends on the schoolyard. As with many of the young boys in his "graduating class," when he graced the makeshift stage, his teacher announced Tay's dream to become an astronaut.

My village of friends cheered wildly as Tay descended the stairs. He faced a major new phase in his life: kindergarten. And on that day he felt loved, supported, and encouraged. He'd never quite settled into naptime, but he'd finally found a place where he was safe to be himself. I took copious photos and hugged him as if he were graduating from a university. I even became tearful when we walked off of the preschool campus. My husband teased me about that.

Before Tay's preschool graduation, I'd filled out the required paperwork with the school district near my new job. Using a work permit allowed me to get into the district, though we didn't live in the area. I got Tay enrolled in a nearby high-performing elementary.

It was a bright ending to preschool. And I had a momentary reprieve from what I've affectionately named Education Stress Syndrome. It's a thing, seriously.

Chapter 5

Parenting is Not for the Weak

Upon visiting Tay's new elementary school, I noticed the quietness and cooperativeness of the kindergarten students. I saw spotless classrooms— a nearly impossible feat in rooms filled with small children. The principal seemed accessible, even chatty. The school had a traditional feel: the building was erected in 1948. And at the top of the list in my uninformed mind, the school had a high API (Academic Performance Index) score.

The API is a measurement of academic performance and progress of individual schools in California. It is one of the main components of the Public Schools Accountability Act passed by the California legislature in 1999. API scores range from a low of 200 to a high of 1,000. Many schools in my home district hovered around the 700 to low 800 API area. The elementary school near my job had a score near 900 and a robust supplemental education program: Lego-robotics classes, music classes, theater, and art. Many of these programs no longer existed at other schools. I believed I had made the perfect choice for Tay. I felt like I was winning as a mom!

But my happy dance was short-lived. Not long after Tay's enrollment in the "perfect" school, the barrage of phone calls to me began. Tay had severe, uncontrollable outbursts. He continued to have angst over transitioning from one activity to the next. On several occasions, I had to leave work early to pick him up or take long phone calls with the teacher and even the principal about his behavior.

It became tough to manage my workload while troubleshooting with my son's teacher about Tay's behavior in class. This school district had a stellar reputation for supporting students. I began to wonder if it was all hype.

***

At the same time, my husband worked longer and longer hours or stayed in the city after hours to meet up with friends. While he came home late practically every night, I contended with school drop-offs and pick-ups and school meetings about how to handle Tay. I felt like a single parent.

To say my husband and I were two ships passing in the night is a stark understatement. We weren't even in the same biosphere. He was concerned about the costs of raising children, and I was concerned about the costs of him not being available to Tay. He invested most of his time in work and work-related friends, and I continued to invest my time into Tay. Our intimacy played out in weekly obligatory late-night connections. No arguments. I wondered if that was a good thing. Our communication was relegated to fake pleasantries at church and family events.

I attempted to resolve our lack of communication. I planned "date nights" that included an entire weekend away. This pitifully unsuccessful endeavor resulted in more of the same.

Over a humble try at a romantic dinner one evening, as I droned on about Tay and his teachers and his issues, my husband said, "I thought we weren't supposed to discuss children during date night." After a moment of suffocating silence, he proceeded to read and send texts on his phone. I stared at him. We had nothing to say to each other. The night ended in complete stillness. Yep, we'd become "that" couple--the kind that only has their kids in common.

I began to imagine my life as a divorcée. I created a budget for my new life as a single mom (with a line item for shoes I'd no longer have to sneak into the house). I wondered how we'd co-parent. Would he use organic products without me around? Would I still be in charge of activities and education? Would he come over to catch and release the bugs that got into the house, especially the spiders? He'd always fearlessly approached them without recoiling, regardless of their size, while I'd screamed like my life was in danger every time a mosquito snuck inside.

These thoughts whirled through my head like a satin bed sheet floating to its spot on a California king mattress. I felt deserted, fatigued, crushed. This was not the life I'd imagined when I exchanged vows with my best friend in the opulent flower garden at the Cleveland country club. This was something painful and completely unforeseen. Clearly, I had no idea how to be a wife after children. And having a child like Tay, who exhibited learning challenges, didn't make it any easier. Rather than discuss the issue, my husband and I simply separated ourselves from each other emotionally. When he came home, he was like a foreigner in the world I'd built with Tay.

But that world was not enough to support Tay's needs. The calls and the meetings escalated. I met with the afterschool staff and talked with his teacher. Everyone reported on Tay's frequent movement around and even outside of the classroom. On some occasions, he ran out of class; on others he sat under his desk during instruction time. When he caused a school toilet to become clogged, he received his first suspension. But it wouldn't be his last.

It seemed like everything around me was falling apart.

***

One day, in the midst of a particularly difficult conversation with Tay's teacher, she explained that she didn't think she could help him. She insinuated he was mentally disturbed, the first time I'd heard anyone refer to my son in that manner. She wanted to know if I had any solutions. I cried during the call. I did not have solutions.

I decided that I had to quit my job. Tay had just started elementary school, and the person tasked with educating him could not. The only other option would be to wait for my performance review, during which I'd surely be told I took too many personal calls, was unfocused, and didn't have a sense of urgency around my work. And it would have been completely true. Quitting seemed doable at the time—not ideal, but feasible. Besides, there were only so many times after a difficult discussion about Tay that I could return to my desk and pretend severe allergies explained my reddened eyes.

Luckily, an empathetic vice president in my department named JB, who also had children, offered his complete support. He listened to me regularly when I needed to vent and fully agreed with my decision to leave the position. "After all," he often said, "the real work starts when you leave this office anyway. It's the kids."

During my last week of work, the president of the company encouraged me, sharing her own story about managing motherhood and her demanding career. Though her son was already an adult, I could still see the fresh abrasions of her choices in her demeanor. I just knew I had the right answer and this decision was going to somehow fix everything—both my marriage and my son. I would have more time for everyone!

As I prepared myself to "retire," I also got ready for my first official meeting with Tay's kindergarten teacher. All our previous discussions had been informal.

She wanted to talk about the possibility of a 504 plan. I had no idea what that was, so I went to the Internet, printed out a bunch of material, and placed it in a folder so I'd appear competent when we met. Years in the entertainment industry had taught me: it's not what you know, but what people think you know.

***

The 504 Plan is supposed to ensure that a child who has a disability identified under the law and is attending an elementary or secondary educational institution receives accommodations that will guarantee his or her academic success. At least that's the jargon used to define it. At that point, I hadn't thought of Tay's behavior as a disability (or a mental disturbance issue). But I was open to all plans, tools, and even magic tricks.

Tay's teacher had an unassuming presence. She seemed young, but then again I'd started my family late in life. Everyone seemed young to me. Tay's teacher explained the slight accommodations in Tay's plan: giving directions in smaller chunks, and utilizing a peer partner to demonstrate proper classroom behavior. The solutions weren't very meaty. That measly plan was supposed to resolve issues with a kid who spent the majority of his day in the principal's office? The 504 didn't seem comprehensive enough for Tay.

There was no mention of academic or psychological testing, no extra support staff, none of the good stuff. It turns out students with 504 plans don't even require specialized instruction. I later learned that many schools start with this plan and stick to it, even if it's not working, because it requires less effort and expense. The 504 plan does not include any legal requirements. Accommodations just have to be "reasonable," and that definition varies per school and per classroom.

In the meantime, all we had for Tay was a one-page piece of paper that was more useful as an airplane than as a guide for educating my son. He struggled in all areas except art. He didn't understand the material presented in class and moved around constantly, which distracted other students. I supported him through playing learning games at home. But it was insufficient.

***

However, one thing did seem to work, at least momentarily. I started dropping Tay off earlier in the mornings. The spacious yard that led to the front door of the school provided him an opportunity to run to class. He ran from one side of the school to the other. After a few weeks of this, the other students cheered for Tay as he sprinted to his building. He loved it. And the physical activity seemed to give him an outlet. According to some school staff members, the morning instruction went a little more smoothly.

By the afternoon, however, Tay walked at inappropriate times, blurted out answers, and sang while the teacher presented her lesson plans. The school's answer was to send him to the principal's office frequently, where he sat until he was released into the afterschool program. He also racked up two school suspensions during his tenure at the school: one the result of stopping the toilet with a banana and the other from leaning back in his chair until he fell.

Soon, I faced the unintended effect of my decision to leave work. Though school administrators had known about my plans ahead of time, the district discharged Tay once they confirmed I no longer had a job within their parameters. Yep, they dumped us and not even to our faces, like that boyfriend who meets someone else and ends the old relationship via text.

They dumped us in a nicely worded letter that I did not expect. In it, the principal even congratulated me on my decision to become a stay-at-home mom. Yet someone at the school had obviously reported my work status to the district office, and now Tay could no longer attend.

But I wouldn't allow myself to get too upset. I didn't have time. Once again, I had to find a new place for Tay.

On to elementary school number two.

***

It was time to think big picture. One smog-filled night, as I walked the neighborhood, the plan came to me and I presented it to my husband. We'd move from our neighborhood so Tay wouldn't be stuck attending our local school. I was still convinced that a good API score was the key to securing a place for him. Maybe it hadn't worked out previously, but a great neighborhood with enormous, handsome houses and excellent school scores had to be a better fit than our mediocre home school in a neighborhood where diminutive starter homes ruled.

I'd heard of a number of families who left their residences and moved into apartments in order to get into "better," if that's what it took. I was willing to do the same; anything short of a studio apartment was fair game (I needed at least one separate room where I could escape everyone for my own sanity.) I was sure I loved my kid as much as those other parents. Our house was just a structure. What mattered most were the people inside. At least that's how I saw things.

As was customary at that point in our marriage, my husband and I were not on the same page. He didn't like the plan. He wasn't on board with my decision to leave work or the sale of our home, but he complied. At that point, silent discontent was better than verbal conflict.

At the end of the calendar year, before the second half of kindergarten began, I called a realtor. We discussed putting our house up for sale so we could rent something in a more prestigious neighborhood. We also wanted something bigger. At age 43, while still nursing our daughter (and without any planning or conception aid whatsoever), I'd somehow become pregnant (completely debunking the old wives' tale that it couldn't happen while nursing).

Simultaneously, my father-in-law's health took a turn for the worse. Our family stress heightened, and I saw my husband even less. He began to jokingly refer to us as roommates (with benefits).

We forged ahead with placing our house on the market. I drove through nearby suburbs, sometimes dragging uncooperative kids along. I sent photos to my mother, who planned to live with us to assist with the third child. I had the goal of identifying a great neighborhood, one with a high-performing elementary school and rental prices that wouldn't give my husband heart palpitations every month when we sent the check to the landlord.

After making some minor changes to our place, we received multiple offers on our home the same week we listed it. That same week, I lost the baby. I returned to work within two days with little time to grieve. I cried when I spoke about her, and I secretly wondered if my internal struggles had somehow contributed to the miscarriage.

The very next month, I lost my father-in-law. When I neglected to fill in my time sheet the day before his funeral, I received a message from the human resources department regarding my missing hours. I fired back an email about the insensitivity it took to send such a message. Adulthood felt too heavy for me to handle, and I longed for my own childhood years swathed in emotional safety.

***

I looked on my own for a place for us to move. Finally, I identified a suitable neighborhood where API scores in the upper 800–900 range abounded. My husband didn't see the place until we moved in. But my excitement over the new beginning became infectious. Tay grew excited over the prospect of having his own room. The novelty of sleeping next to his sister had worn off. My husband liked the size of the backyard. My excitement still came from living in a neighborhood with high-performing schools. From my vantage point, I'd hit the mother lode. I high-fived myself and reported back to my friends and family about finding the figurative key to Tay's success.

The determination to get something right had finally paid off. I slept easier than I had in weeks, despite the fact that we had to pack boxes with ten years of stuff we mostly never used, like the electric potato peeler, vintage mixing-bowl set, and scrapbooking kit.

But life, unpredictable as ever, had more slings and arrows in store for us. It wasn't long before the realization that our move was not the end of Tay's kindergarten problems. Instead, it was the precursor to the showdown.

Chapter 6

My Own Bigtime Bubble Burst

Nestled in the foothills of the Santa Susana Mountains stood a large, mid-century elementary school full of promise. The surrounding community consisted mostly of retired people; many of the homes overlooked a generous golf course. The campus teemed with commuters who traveled large distances, fueled by hopes of a better education than their home schools provided.

I carried into this new mecca my unused, dust-drenched wedding china and my own hopes for my son. I also brought along my mother. Though we'd recruited her to move in with us when we thought there would be a third addition to the family, she came even after we lost the baby. I felt it was best that she moved in to help with Tay.

She'd previously done a brief tour of duty with Tay right after he was born, and with a master's degree in education and years of experience, her expertise superseded what my husband or I could provide. Better still, due to early retirement, she was totally free!

I also thought helping to take care of Tay would give my mother something to focus on. My stepfather had died tragically in a car accident soon after they married, and years later the loss still affected her tremendously.

No one was more excited about Grandma moving in than Tay. They had a special bond that continues even now.

On the first day of school, I clasped Tay's tiny hand until I delivered my curly red haired 5-year old kindergartner to his new teacher, an older, reedy woman who I imagined was nearing retirement. Tay was excited about the adventure we'd started. The principal had been informed about his arrival.

Before we'd left for school that morning, my mother insisted I give them her version of her grandson's capabilities.

"Lia, did you tell them about my grandchild? Did you tell them he's a genius?"

When I'd called the school to enroll him, I hadn't mentioned Tay's genius. I had explained that he had a 504 plan from his previous school. During my conversation with the principal, she assured me our child was in good hands, that the school was full of capable staff adept at handling "all sorts of children." But I'd later find out her assurances were about as honest as a seasoned used-car salesman's nonsense spiel.

***

Within weeks after Tay started his new kindergarten, I found myself dragging him from our front door to the silver Honda minivan every morning to cart him off to class. In fact, each new day he seemed more apprehensive about going to school. I initially attributed his reluctance to the fact that our one-year-old daughter had the privilege of staying home with my mother. Although our new living situation was not without its own trials (the least of which was my mother insisting on treating me as if I were still a teenager living on the second floor of her house), I knew how much the children loved their grandmother.

Grandma made homemade popcorn, let the children color on the walls, and even knew all the words to most pop songs as well as most of the dances that accompanied them. She also line-danced with our daughter, who did the Cha Cha Slide flawlessly before she could talk.

But despite Grandma's appeal, it wasn't leaving her behind that made Tay so hesitant to go to school. A genuine problem lurked behind his classroom door—and it was weeks before I discovered it.

One day, Tay's new teacher stopped me in the doorway, in front of other parents, to tell me how poorly he was doing in school. When I asked what she meant, she told me he sang a lot. I explained that he used music to soothe himself, had done so since he was an infant, and often made up his own songs as well. His teacher insisted his "noise" was just disruptive; she'd never heard anything original out of him, and he was just being silly. He also spent a lot of time under his desk.

Because of these infractions, she suggested I put him on medication for ADHD. Teachers aren't supposed to suggest medication as an option to parents, as they're not doctors. She said she'd read his records from his previous school, and he was obviously troubled.

I realized she'd used the information I armed her with as ammunition to shoot down my son's self-esteem.

I explained that we wanted to keep exploring all on the table, including therapy. I didn't know enough about the long-term effects of medicating a five-year-old to make a determination at that time. Further, I'd seen so many articles about the over-diagnosis of ADHD. Perhaps her assessment of Tay was wrong. Maybe he actually had anxiety or depression. Maybe he had none of those, but a developmental delay instead. Could it be Asperger's? Or obsessive-compulsive disorder? Or something the medical community hadn't named yet? We spoke for several minutes without coming to a resolution.

I decided to ask the principal for an evaluation to determine the problem. But the principal supported her teacher. She refused to do any testing outside of having a resource instructor assess him academically. That instructor determined that Tay did work at grade level. Therefore, he didn't qualify for further examination or support. I found this response peculiar, as I knew he'd struggled in a number of areas when I'd conducted my own informal assessment. Again, I had no clue why, but he didn't seem to grasp the material when we did homework.

The resource teacher also insisted Tay's behavior was purposeful. And even though the classroom teacher suggested he had ADHD, she continued to treat him like a child who simply chose to misbehave. Unlike at his previous school, no one thought he had a learning disability. Their indifference confused me.

I conducted more research and spoke to people I knew in the educational field about how to help Tay. That's when I discovered the IEP (Individualized Education Program).

***

"The IEP is a written document required for each child who is eligible to receive special education services. It is provided to a student who has been determined first to have a disability and, second, to need special education services because of that disability." (US Department of Education)

I was reluctant to think of Tay as "disabled." But that was the logical explanation for his behavior. I requested formal testing to determine if he was eligible for an IEP. The district denied me.

A few of my friends suggested I have Tay tested privately. They thought it was a bad idea to have anything on his record that could be perceived as negative or that would make him stand out. I explained that my son spent a good portion of his classroom experience under or standing on top of his desk. He pretty much already stood out.

He was also a minority in his suburban school who "misbehaved." He'd already been suspended instead of receiving the full support he required, and he'd been labeled as "bad." But children who have undiagnosed learning disabilities tend to be frustrated and may be unable to articulate their feelings of inadequacy—especially in lower elementary. A teacher can misread exasperation over not being able to grasp the material as acts of defiance.

Furthermore, in recent years, studies conducted around teacher bias in the classroom show that boys are more likely to be disciplined than girls. And in the school-to-prison pipeline research, studies have found that black children have a higher probability of suspensions, for the same behavior, as their white counterparts. I began to wonder if there was bias toward my son (intentional or unintentional).

Whatever biases were at play; one truth came into focus: educators often miss opportunities when they don't consider behavior as an indication of a learning disability. I believed Tay's new kindergarten teacher had inappropriately addressed his unorthodox behavior. I needed to find an ally.

Chapter 7

Beginning to Think I Suck at This Job

Unfortunately, I didn't uncover everything that happened at Tay's new kindergarten until I enrolled Tay in counseling. It was then that the pieces of his school-woes puzzle began to fit together.

Tay's therapist told me that he probably did have ADHD, but that he also suffered from a great deal of anxiety. She believed a majority of the anxiety actually stemmed from the treatment he received in his kindergarten class. As Tay became more comfortable with the therapist, he also became more at ease about sharing with me. He reported what had happened in class and how he felt about it.

His therapist used a combination of play therapy and traditional models to evaluate Tay. In the psychological field, the perception is that young children are not good at articulating their feelings, so the best way to connect with them is to play games. Tay and his therapist played with Legos because that was a hobby he enjoyed. They also played with dolls, assigning emotions to them. I told her I did have an evaluation conducted by a private psychologist. But she thought Tay had been over-diagnosed and referred me to a psychiatrist in her agency.

After I filled out my own evaluation, a psychiatrist assessed Tay. Within weeks, we met with the doctor, who concluded Tay had ADHD. I had to accept it (though in the back of my head I wanted to believe his challenges in school stemmed from misunderstood genius). On the one hand, I felt relieved to have an answer. Conversely, I felt confusion over the choices I had to make: medication or not, special learning facility or not, ignoring the diagnosis or not.

ADHD presents problems with impulse control, organization, and social maturity. However, the same rapid-fire thoughts that incited Tay's outside-the-box actions might be the well of brilliance that forges an exciting career path for him one day. He is in the company of greatness, sharing his diagnosis with Will Smith, Michael Phelps, Justin Timberlake, Jamie Oliver, Karina Smirnoff, Paul Orfalea (Kinko's founder), David Neeleman (JetBlue Airways founder) and many others. While ignoring it could not resolve the problem, focusing on it as a detriment to his success could not either.

Tay's therapist told me that in a different school environment, with a teacher who cared about him, he would thrive. He was smart. In fact, he probably was gifted. While his ADHD would have to be managed, she was clear on Tay's many attributes—speaking, creativity, music—and said he was "emotionally articulate." She explained that getting under the table or leaving the classroom were his own methods of regulating his body when he felt overwhelmed. His kindergarten teacher had thought those were acts of defiance from a troubled boy. The therapist saw the opposite: his behavior showed a keen level of awareness and desire to conform. She wanted to help us get through the layers of trauma she believed encouraged his negative behavior.

I didn't expect to change his teacher. But we did have to get through the rest of the school year.

***

I soon discovered the staff at his new school was even less supportive than the staff at the previous one. Tay's teacher was also divisive and combative, isolating Tay in ways that would damage him through the next year. He began to question his intelligence and refer to himself as a kid with problems.

One day when Tay had an especially hard time sitting in class, his teacher organized a classroom vote on whether or not he deserved to attend another child's birthday party. She also said he was the worst child she'd ever taught and told another black student, in Tay's presence, he would end up in jail. That stinging pronouncement traumatized Tay, who later asked me, "what kind of kids go to jail?"

He feared being locked away for months. When he originally asked me about jail that year, I thought maybe he'd heard something from another student. I had no idea his teacher had brought up the concept of incarceration.

Unfortunately, I learned about these things much too late. In the moment, I was unaware of all the distress his teacher had caused or the long-term effect it would have on my son because I was struggling with my own issues. I was in the midst of figuring out a path to a future career that aligned with motherhood and my creativity, overcoming the loss of my surprise pregnancy, and dealing with the death of my father-in-law.

I dropped the Mommy ball and it crashed into a big wall. Despite the red flags, I still wanted to believe that Tay's new school could work for us. Its scores were high. It sat among prime real estate in a neighborhood with hardly any crime, unless you counted the occasional bear stealing a dip in a neighbor's pool. The school had to be the place where Tay could thrive.

As I had been many times as a mother (and would be again in the future), I was way off.

During our unfortunate time at that school, another mother (who happened to be the PTA president) was actively pursuing a lawsuit because she said her son's teacher slapped him. He was a special-education student; the teacher alleged that he bit her. Even if that were true, her response was clearly inappropriate. But the principal sided with the teacher. So what I encountered should not have been a surprise. I wasn't even an active member of the PTA.

Eventually, I fully accepted the realization that the source of Tay's aversion to school. I believed the way his teacher treated him had heightened his behavior problems instead of reducing them. Tay's teacher spoke to him inappropriately, made fun of him, and repeatedly rallied other students against him. When I asked to have a private meeting with her after school, without other students and parents listening and judging, she continually hid behind her unavailability. Even though it was near the end of the school year, I had to shift things and quickly.

Although Taylor was only six, we formed a partnership around his education, and I finally asked him about transferring to yet another school. Initially, I'd been opposed to making such a drastic change, as he'd already been in so many different places in his short educational career. Tay told me, "If I left my school, I would miss my friends. And I won't have a chance to get my teacher to like me."

He'd been drawing pictures for her and making cards for her so that she'd come around.

Talk about a sucker punch to a mom's gut. I was devastated. I'd failed him miserably. Even he was aware of how his teacher felt about him. And I felt like I really sucked at being a mom; I'd left one of my most valuable treasures unprotected.

I ached for my son's hurts. He was sensitive, kind, and acutely misunderstood. His teacher never recognized his gift of music, his sense of humor, or his kind heart. As a matter of fact, she didn't know him at all. I wasn't the only one who missed things. She'd missed the most important things, and that continued to fuel my anger.

***

Equipped with my private test results, I made a more formalized request to have my son tested for academic services in school.

I also met with the school principal to report the teacher's abhorrent behavior and to follow-up on my IEP request. She informed me that my second request for assessments in order to obtain an IEP had been denied. Further, she didn't believe Tay's instructor had directed any hurtful words specifically at him. Totally disconnected from the situation, with a mere few months before leaving her job, the principal had nothing to offer but for me to transfer out of her school.

"If you don't like it here," she quipped, "I suggest you pull your son out."

That option made no sense. Pull him out to go where? Tay was enrolled in our district-assigned school with just weeks left in the school year. Maybe I could try to get everyone fired somehow, or like the mother suing the school, I could call the local news channels and start my own social-media campaign. But that also made no sense. Investing my energy in character assassinations ultimately didn't seem like the best use of time.

Still, I wasn't going to let things go. I couldn't. So, I got some help from someone who knew way more about uncooperative school administrators than I did. I got my own personal superhero.

Chapter 8

The Superhero Wears Prada

After being denied twice, I had to get help with my pursuit of an IEP. For a student like Tay, this single document packs a lot of punch. Designed specifically to meet the educational needs of the student, it guarantees substantial supports and services that everyone agrees upon, including the parents. So I wanted one like a reality star wants air time.

The IEP must include both strengths and needs, academic as well as in any other areas of concern such as language development, behavior, or social skills. (Behavior and social skills happened to be Tay's main struggles.) The document also outlines goals the student can reasonably accomplish in one year.

According to law, the IEP must contain a plan for measuring and reporting on the student's progress toward those annual goals. That was exactly what Tay needed. What's more, a student performing at grade level is not disqualified from getting an IEP. Bingo!

The best part about establishing an IEP is that once it's written, the school district is obligated to provide "a free appropriate public education (FAPE) in the least restrictive environment (LRE)." So the IEP team (which includes the parents) has to figure out how to educate the student alongside kids without a disability. The district is required by law to provide the services to support the IEP. Such services can be costly, and I believe that's the reason some requests for IEPs are rejected. It may very well be one of the reasons both of my requests were denied. It may have had nothing to do with Tay as a student at all.

Armed with this information, I knew it was necessary to find someone who could ensure our request for an IEP was not refused again—

someone a lot more qualified than me. So, the research began. And then the writing.

***

I'm not the type of person who starts altercations. Instead, I quietly express my discontent in letters. I started to explore this non-confrontational form of conflict resolution sometime during elementary school when a girl wanted to meet me at 3 p.m. on the playground. She wanted to fight, and I hated fighting. Even in the third grade, it seemed like an ignorant way to resolve problems.

Instead, I began to write letters to people when they upset me. By college, I perfected the art of letter writing and employed it for break-ups, make-ups, and other communications that required diplomacy. Eventually, I took over the editorial section of the university newspaper where I could write endless letters from week to week, voicing my opinion on anything I cared about.

I've written to colleagues, restaurant owners, bank managers, and even sent a barrage of correspondence to the State Tax Board when they claimed a portion of my pay that year belonged to them. So it was no different dealing with my son's second elementary school administration. I documented everything. I then folded my emotional damage and the facts of our experience into an email. Soon after sending it off to a local special-education attorney with a reputation for wins against our school district (we'll call her Attorney V), we had a meeting in place.

***

Attorney V's capacious, well-appointed office was evidence of her success at what she did. And I'm pretty sure I spotted a designer bag in the corner with a price tag higher than my rent. Most importantly, she wore a classic dark skirt—something I'd been taught in my young executive days symbolized confidence and power. Who knows if it's true, but that kind of thing stuck with me. Most importantly, after I talked to Attorney V, I appreciated how passionate she was about her work.

Attorney V assured me my local school district administrators were very familiar with her legal firm. Immediately, I knew I was in competent hands. That assuaged my anxiety. I felt comfortable sharing all of the information about Tay I had at my disposal. After I told her about my denied IEP requests, she said, "Yeah, they pull that kind of thing sometimes, but the district knows me and they will comply."

The stack of material I brought, including the psychiatrist's assessments and documentation recounting Tay's treatment by the staff in his school, covered her desk. The attorney quickly read over the material as she rocked a little in her leather executive chair and uttered an occasional "uh" or "oooh."

By the time our meeting took place, at least five other parents of children with special needs had either filed their own lawsuits against the same school or planned to do so. I told my attorney that as well.

Attorney V pushed aside Tay's records and helped me craft a letter to the school district that day in her office. It was brief and direct but authoritative. When I left that Sherman Oaks building, I felt a little more settled about Tay's future.

I delivered the letter to the school principal before the end of the school year. It included language that acknowledged the school staff was not adhering to Tay's original 504 plan from his first kindergarten. It also stated that the school had not agreed to comply with my initial request for a more comprehensive plan in the form of an IEP. Concurrently, I lodged complaints with the local school board and the Special Education Department of California. I also contacted a local parent advocacy organization. At this point, I was so angry that I complained to anyone who had anything to do with education within a reasonable radius of Southern California.

My intent was never to engage in a legal battle. I wanted my son to have access to a fair and appropriate education (now that I'd finally learned about it). It is the right of every child in the United States.

I also wanted people to know that his school was unwilling to provide that education, and that I knew Tay wasn't the only victim of this toxic environment. Many parents don't know their rights and may not have access to an attorney. In some small way, I felt like I was becoming a voice for those people, too—a loud, irritating voice that would not go gently.

***

In the meantime, as Tay finished his last weeks of the school year, it became clear to me that he had even more trouble sitting for long periods of time and his anxiety was increasing, despite therapeutic intervention. He still ran out of class on occasion and sat under his desk (or the teacher's) and sang during instruction time. He played with small items in his hand or found coarse surfaces to stroke while he worked. All of these behaviors seemed to exasperate the teacher, who frequently complained about them.

Even though his school would finally be forced to adhere to my request for an IEP, I was certain that the staff was incapable of teaching my child. No one had noticed that he was trying to control his anxiety and over-stimulation, as the therapist had said. He tried to calm himself down using whatever was around him—something many children do when their bodies don't self soothe naturally. I learned more about other children like this when I watched a documentary about students with sensory-integration problems. One of the students in the film reminded me of my son.

Sensory integration is the ability to take in sensory information from our bodies and the environment and organize it for effective, functional participation in daily activities. This process is automatic when it works correctly. The problems arise when the process is disrupted and neither parents nor educators identify the issue.

While the parents of children with sensory-integration problems see the effects, some psychologists and educators don't believe the condition is real. In Tay's case, his teacher just thought he was being "silly," and her principal backed her up. It was frustrating.

I poured all of my energy into research on IEPs and schools that might be appropriate for someone like my kid. He needed an environment that could provide him structure in a positive way. I didn't know where this enchanted school might be, but I was again determined to discover it.

In the meantime, I made a request to the principal for Tay be removed from his classroom. I thought that might be a temporary fix until he transferred somewhere else altogether. Unexpectedly, she complied (having ignored every other request I'd made). But the new situation was not much better.

The new teacher already had an opinion about my little boy before he arrived. The culture of the school was to share students' private information with other teachers as well as other parents. So changing classrooms did not resolve the problem. Instead, we found ourselves facing a different teacher with a different type of dysfunction.

I visited Tay's class nearly every day at this point. According to his 504 plan, he was supposed to be seated in the front, near the teacher. Instead, he sat in the back. Many teachers place their problematic students in the back of the classroom to get them out of the way, but that's the opposite of what these children need.

When I asked for a meeting with his new teacher, she had no time for me (though it seemed she found time to flirt with the male parents for several minutes after school each afternoon). She yelled as a form of "managing" her students and allowed children to physically attack each other without intervening. I witnessed one child pull another to the ground by her ponytail. When I reported it, the teacher told me, "They just have a love-hate relationship."

When I asked if I could help my little genius in class, the principal told me it wouldn't be appropriate. Further, since his teacher wouldn't give him detailed instructions or allow him extra time to complete his work, he couldn't keep up with the coursework. The situation got so heated at one point, I considered inviting this new teacher to the schoolyard to handle things. But we had to push through those last few weeks of the school year.

It seemed neither one of his teachers wanted to make the slightest accommodations for kids like my child. Totally distracted by the chaos in the room, he repeatedly disengaged. His new teacher's desk was so cluttered, I would have had a hard time focusing, too! I referred to it as the Leaning Tower of Pisa.

I finally cornered the new instructor to discuss Tay's issues after class. She seemed vacant and uninterested. I could've been talking about the number of dandelions on campus as far as she was concerned. I felt like I was up against a mean girl in high school who had a club I couldn't join.

I quickly became exasperated by this going-nowhere conversation. My voice quivered so much she called the principal to the classroom (I guess she needed backup). I stood inches away from her, ready to scream my demands into her impassive face, when I realized there were students nearby. I paused; I had to exercise the same tolerance I begged the staff at this very school to exercise with Tay. I coached myself in my head: "Be patient and kind."

I took a deep affirming breath, silently counted to three, imagined lounging in a spa, and stepped back. But a few words escaped my mouth without my full consent, "If he were your son ..." I began, finger pointed inches from her nose, grasping for some sort of empathy. My entire body shuddered. Then I exited the room backward as if in a country western, ending a face-off in the town saloon.

I passed the aggravated principal on my way off the campus. I told her she should be ashamed of the culture at her school. Again, she suggested I consider pulling Tay out of the school. The romanticized future I'd crafted for Tay before we moved into that suburban sanctuary had been completely destroyed.

I felt like a seriously mediocre mom.

***

During the final days of the school year, I continued to go into the classroom to watch Tay almost every day. I stayed clear of all staff members. I took profuse notes on Tay's behavior and the responses from the teacher. Though I was not allowed to assist Tay, the school could not prevent me from observing him. And my presence did mitigate any bullying on the part of his teacher. His new teacher completely ignored him. The lesser evil.

Sometimes Tay forgot I was there and just let loose. Those were actually the most helpful times for me. I could take comprehensive notes about any difficult behavior and what happened just before it began.

The teacher's yelling subsided (She never forgot I was there.) I documented everything. Tay's school observation file became thicker than Tolstoy's War and Peace.

My mother also sat in on his class occasionally. Her background in education as both a teacher and guidance counselor added another perspective.

Looking back, my mother and I were probably both holding onto hope that there might be a way to resolve things without disrupting Tay yet again. Neither of us wanted to pull him out of another school. But it was not the place for Tay, or any child who learned differently. Nothing would change that fact.

I hired a tutor for Tay so that, despite what happened in the classroom, he had a positive teacher-student relationship with someone. The tutor used games and incentives with Tay and made learning enjoyable. Sometimes, Tay had a hard time focusing despite his instructor's creative learning tools. So I developed a few tools such as having Tay walk to me while spelling words, and making trails of vocabulary notecards that lined the walls of our home.

The tutor's reputation as a competent instructor spread around the school and other parents hired her as well. Unfortunately for us, her skills eventually got her picked up by the school district full time. She could no longer tutor.

My husband and I decided that for Tay, the last days of school would just be about socializing. I worked with the tutor as long as we had her to cover education. I continued to come up with ways to keep Tay on task. He wrote for five minutes, then ran around the backyard in a circle five times (Of course, he loved the running part.) He had an incentive chart with fun animal stickers he could earn. And once in a while we took a trip to the local yogurt store as a reward for productive sessions.

I also pulled Tay out of the afterschool program and began spending more one-on-one time with him. I adjusted his diet as much as I could. The limitations in this area made it difficult because he had heightened sensory sensitivity around food. Many textures and smells bothered him. But I increased his protein intake by giving him shakes infused with veggies, and I limited his carbs.

Tay's therapist was a huge help. She pointed out that his length of sleep time needed to change. So I put him to bed earlier and I worked with him on a bedroom routine. I typed and pasted the new schedule on a wall with clip art and colorful fonts. We also practiced breathing through his stressful moments and being aware of his actions and their long-term consequences. I asked him what he thought would happen if he flipped a chair in anger. Could he hurt someone? Could he hurt himself? Could he break the chair? How would that feel? This helped my son process through challenges he faced.

I signed Tay up for a few social-skills classes and periodically took him to a local play gym called "We Rock the Spectrum." The gym specialized in supporting children with learning differences. It became one of the few places where Tay could be himself without being constantly corrected. Sadly, I admit, that didn't even happen in his own home.

***

After speaking with the attorney a number of times and engaging in frequent conversations with special-needs professionals, I was told about options for Tay like charter and magnet schools. I mailed applications to three magnet schools and a plethora of private schools. We spent hundreds of dollars on fees, and I spent hours on school visits and interviews. Many private-school directors were kind and nonjudgmental toward us, but heads of schools and directors unanimously told me that public school was probably the best fit for Tay. They had far more supports if we could get them. It just had to be the right place.

I created back-up plans for my back-up plans to get out of our home school into a school with a more tolerant climate. I even applied to a coveted charter that specialized in children with learning differences. But we didn't get in. And he got waitlisted for a local progressive private school after they observed him in class. They were looking for diversity—just not that type of diversity.

One school administrator told us their level of academics could be problematic for him, and another just never returned any phone calls. I felt completely defeated. I really didn't know where Tay would end up.

Then I received a phone call one afternoon from our school district coordinator. Our school district is so large that there are units set up to address the complaints of parents. They are divided geographically. The coordinator assigned to my neighborhood had the copy of the letter I'd crafted with my attorney. It painted broad strokes about Tay's kindergarten experience and the legal language needed to remind the district about due process.

Due process hearing proceedings are dispute-resolution proceedings required to be available to parents and school districts by the Individuals with Disabilities Education Act (IDEA). Parents can file a due process complaint on any matter relating to a proposal or refusal to initiate or change a student's identification, evaluation, or educational placement. It's the last resort for parents who aren't getting what they need from their school district. Most parents don't want an adversarial relationship with their district, but if their child's needs are not being served, it might be the only path to resolution.

In our school district, parents have three options: Informal Dispute Resolution (IDR), State Mediation, or Formal Due Process Proceedings. Due Process is the lengthiest and the costliest.

By the time I received the district coordinator's phone call, I'd forgotten I'd even forwarded the letter of grievances to him. I'd looked up his name when I was searching for people who might be able to address my complaints about Tay's elementary school.

The coordinator seemed a little frazzled but assured me everything was going to be fine. I expected the school district to agree with my request because it came from an attorney. But when their acquiesce finally happened, it still felt surreal. The coordinator told me Tay qualified to receive an assessment for an IEP. An appointment was made for Tay to get tested over the summer. Further, he'd been enrolled in one of the magnet schools to which I'd applied. Overcome with happiness, I hung up the phone and screamed as if I had won the lotto. Because I had.

A wave of relief crashed through my fatigued joints and I finally felt like I'd accomplished a significant win. My attorney had done her job. My kid was going to have a better school experience in the fall. And I felt like one area of my life was coming to a resolution.

But another was still slipping through my fingers.

Chapter 9

A Joke and a Prayer

In the midst of all the ups and downs of my son's educational journey, I felt a huge loss—that loss being me. All of my waking energy seemed to be shifted toward my son. I mean, I love the kid, but he couldn't become my whole life. I began to think about areas I'd always wanted to explore. That life exploration led me to a class–a stand-up comedy class.

I wanted to get back into writing comedy because that was the original reason I moved to Los Angeles in my twenties. I started writing jokes back in junior high, and—you guessed it—when I came out of my shell in high school, I turned into one of those jokesters that the teachers didn't care very much about. I ended up paying for my smart mouth in detention. But that's another story.

I wrote my first comedy script in college, a spec (writing sample) episode of The Fresh Prince of Bel Air. I wrote my first stand-up routine in my early twenties about dating in LA, but a TV agent discouraged me from taking the stage. "No one thinks a cute girl talking about dating troubles is funny," he said. He had no idea about my tragically dismal dating choices. Pure comedy.

When I walked into the room where the class met (basically a cheerleading session), I had a large measure of skepticism. The first assignment was to tell the class about a humiliating moment we'd experienced.

To my mind, it's difficult for a forty-something woman to be humiliated. At that point in life, I just didn't give a crap anymore. I mean, I'd had a baby at a "teaching hospital," which meant an audience of students shared my delivery with me. Virtual strangers saw more of my body parts than my husband had over our entire ten-year marriage.

But I eventually remembered something embarrassing—a relationship break-up in college. There'd been lots of them, but one was particularly ridiculous. I painted a picture of me chasing a man down fifteen flights of stairs to ask, "Why! Why!" on a busy Chicago street, with on-lookers shaking their heads while my slobbering drool mixed with the mucus running down my face. When my cheating-air-force-pilot-eight-years-my-senior boyfriend took off in silver BMW, I went back to open the front door of my apartment. But I hadn't managed to bring my keys along for the chase. It would be hours before I got into my apartment and days before I met the next boyfriend.

My classmates laughed at my overly dramatized retelling of the dys-functional demise of that union. A euphoric feeling settled my pounding heart. I realized why people did this, why they took the risk of being emotionally naked in front of complete strangers. I wanted to do it again. So I did. Often.

***

After a few weeks of class, my teacher strongly encouraged us to perform our stand-up routines at open mics. An addictive hobby turned into a lifestyle. Some nights I tested jokes at two or three open mics (and on friends and family or the neighborhood grocery-store clerk).

I began building material around my husband and the issues I en-countered with my son, and my shows got better. Not only that, I shifted my viewpoint by digging through life's rubble for humor. Life became funny. I felt like the issues seemed less daunting.

The stage provided me with a place to dump, leaving room for me to discuss other things with my husband. It became my release, my therapy, and my way to put my experiences in perspective. I needed something that was just mine, and the stage was it.

I also found another tool—prayer. I began to pray about my son, my career, my husband, and to operate as if things worked in a healthy way. My prayers were about gratitude. Every morning I meditated on what I had.

Prayer transformed the way I looked at everything. I pushed for me and my husband to have real date nights and encouraged conversations about pointless things like the alcohol-induced advice I received from other comics or the latest rant on The Daily Show.

I decided to delete the single-mother budget file I'd created that night in anger. I no longer complained about the lack of support I received from my spouse. Instead, I articulated the gaps in our relationship and suggested ways they could be filled: a consistent babysitter, help with laundry, attendance at an IEP meeting.

Ironically, I received the most encouragement and direction from my husband's cousin, a talented artist and mother who'd always seemed to get me. Some would say we were cut from the same artistic cloth. After a myriad talks with her and a few visits to a marriage counselor, I became the change I wanted. And I began to focus on meeting my husband's needs. Wired to be independent through my upbringing by a single mom, I admit catering to my man did not feel intuitive. But it began to feel right for me.

I had to act like a girlfriend, like we'd just met. I placed notes in his lunches, showed up unexpectedly for office "dates," and made sure I publicly complimented my husband. For a while, I had to pretend. It was difficult. At times, I didn't even like my husband very much. Marriage, like parenting, is a selfless act. It requires an enormous amount of forgiveness. I didn't know if I had the right stuff to do what it took to stay. But, eventually, my husband changed too. He reciprocated. He planned dates. He helped more with our children. He prayed for me. I no longer felt isolated. We became friends again. Over time, neither of us remembered why we were so angry with each other.

But I did have to give something up. Just as my husband had felt an abandonment when I took on motherhood, he felt deserted when I took to comedy. Meanwhile, my mother purchased a house back in Las Vegas. She'd no longer help fill in the holes of my absences. I had to be home. But at least the home was filled with laughs.

Comedy was my zen, a therapeutic space. I believe all parents who have a child with a special need should have something to turn to for calm. It might be race-car driving, rollerblading, singing, writing, taking classes in a new field, or any number of other things, but it's important.

For me, there have been some incredible nights performing stand-up, including the opportunity to audition for Nickelodeon. One of my favorite nights took place five weeks after I first took the stage. At around eleven that night, I stood outside of The Improv, Hollywood with Rawle D, a local comedian. Rather than changing a soaked diaper or cleaning my son's urine off the bathroom wall, I stood in a circle of established professionals as if I belonged there.

We talked comedy shop with that night's headliner—Theo Von, a successful, full-time, employed comedian. In the midst of our laughing and joking, Theo said, "We should all do a show together" and my friend Rawle D said, "Yeah, we should."

For a girl who grew up in a tiny suburb of Cleveland, it was amazing to me to have ever performed at The Improv, one of the oldest and most legendary clubs in Los Angeles, and to be in the company of real comics as an equal. I had many fun times during my short tenure in that world. But there's no reason I can't go back to it. As with many mom comedians, that time will just have to arrive when my children are out of the house. In the meantime, I had to focus in strengthening a new skill–advocacy.

Chapter 10

Time for a Change: Our IEP

My father once told me that in almost every situation, "behavior is a symptom, not the disease. Find the source of the behavior, you can cure the disease."

I discovered through research and painstaking trial and error that the primary source of my son's behavior might not ever be "cured." But ADHD could be managed.

Once our appointment for assessments was confirmed, I explained to Tay before testing why it needed to be done. Even though we had our own tests from the psychologist and psychiatrist, our school district had to conduct their assessments before providing any support in school.

I assured Tay testing would be quick. Then we'd get to the rest of the summer, which included typical fun like camp and trips to the park or visiting family members. What made summer challenging for us was that by that point, TV watching had been relegated to weekends only, owing to my concern over excessive media in our home. So the time we usually spent on homework during the week had to be filled up with other things. I bought board games (and made up my own), we played cards, and we went to the park. Taylor also enjoyed running with his father.

Since Tay loved TV (and still does), by Saturday he woke up at 5:00 a.m. to get started. He also had a routine that we affectionately named the "imaginative download." Before running to turn on the television, Tay stood over our bed, eager to rattle off a glut of his dreamed-up stories.

After he finished, Tay's Saturday morning TV time gave us the breather we needed. Most Saturdays, neither I nor my husband had the energy to engage our son that early, so we capitulated to child-friendly programming as our sitter. As loud as the TV was, his sister slept right through it. She clearly takes after me that way.

By late Saturday mornings, we took up our schedule of physical, educational, and therapeutic activities. I'd realized Tay was gifted in music; he'd been singing on key since age two. I wanted to continue to encourage music as an outlet for him, so I found a music therapy class at a local college. He connected very well with the instructor. Eventually, I also found a special-needs basketball league where Tay could play without pressure. The league's founder had a vision of special-needs children of all faiths playing sports together. He set a tone of love and encouragement.

Even over the summer, sitting for long periods was difficult for Tay, and so was staying organized. I put up more lists with pictures depicting his activities and chores: put toys away, put your shoes away, clean your room, bring in the mail, and so on.

As I came to understand my son better, I grew more confident communicating to others how best to manage him. His camp experience improved because his counselor exhibited an extra measure of patience. She also discovered the magic of Tay and Play-Doh; manipulating it seemed to calm him. But when that didn't succeed, I picked him up early. Many days, things went well.

However, the final test would come at Tay's new school. Summer, albeit challenging at times, was the easy part.

**

Within one week after first grade began, I received a phone call from the new principal at Tay's magnet school. He'd received my son's assessments and already had comprehensive feedback from his new teacher. I really liked him. He'd been assistant principal at a nearby school for gifted kids, so he was accustomed to handling children who expressed themselves in non-traditional ways.

I told the new principal about my availability as a full-time mom. I was "all in" on my son's education.

And then it happened. We set up a time to meet. The very next week. I was going to have my first official IEP meeting. I was psyched like I'd just won a pair of Adele concert tickets. After coming from a frustrating place where I couldn't get a meeting even after several requests, I was impressed with this school. They really seemed to want to help Tay.

Admittedly, the thought of sitting with a bunch of experts in the assistant principal's (AP) office intimidated me a little. In our district, the AP oversees the special-needs program in the school. APs are assigned up to four schools, so they're not always able to have intimate relationships with parents. But this school encouraged a clear line of communication with families, despite the AP's workload.

Our AP was thoughtful, sensitive, and knowledgeable about current trends in education. She wanted me to be prepared to take in the information placed in front of me, a thirty-eight-page document about my son. On first sight, it just looked like a hugely daunting stack of paper. But it was Tay's IEP.

Our AP said they'd needed to document his most egregious behavior in order to request the highest level of services for him. The IEP included Tay's refusal to stay in class the entire time, his turning over of furniture, and his inability to grasp the curriculum taught in class, landing him two grades below grade level by the time he got assessed. Either everything he'd learned in kindergarten had somehow vanished from his memory, or the previous school's class had been a lot less challenging than I thought. When I read the IEP, I was overcome with sadness—and again, a feeling of incompetence.

The AP sensed my heart palpitations and explained that they were going to do everything in their power to get the accommodations I requested. "He's a great boy and we just want him to succeed," she said.

Another first. An educator who actually thought—and said out loud—that my son was "great." I hadn't heard Tay described in such positive terms by anyone in any school he'd ever attended. I'd heard "defiant," "aggressive," "disrespectful" … but never "GREAT."

I learned that IEP meetings can elicit many emotions for parents because the focus is on the disability or behavior that's preventing the child from thriving. But no one has a better perspective on my son than I do. I knew there was much more to Taylor than what was in that paperwork.

***

When the meeting ended, I decided to take the IEP home to review it. First, I poured a glass of wine. I opted for red and went online. I had to look up many of the document's terms on the Internet and I asked people I knew in the education field to explain certain things to me. I even signed up for a class on understanding IEPs, taught by a local attorney. But I didn't want to delay progress, waiting for that class to start. I signed the IEP. At last, my son was going to get everything from counseling services to a one-to-one aide.

Schools assign one-to-one-aides to children for various reasons: behavior management, instructional support, activities of daily living (e.g. toileting, dressing, hygiene), social-skills training, task redirection, and more. My son needed that support because he needed breaks. As a 6-year-old, he had to have an adult take him out of class when necessary. I hoped this would prevent the under-the-desk episodes of years past.

Though the promise of a one-to-one aide was the most significant part of my son's support services, I knew the process of actually securing one could take a while. We're in one of the largest school districts in the country, where sometimes it seems everything takes about fifty times longer than expected plus another three weeks. So I came up with a plan. After discussing it with my husband, I decided to join my son in first grade. I would become his one-to-one aide.

I emailed my son's first-grade teacher to offer my services as his aide. Beyond thrilled, she expressed her gratitude. And I prepared my son for my new job, working for him.

But I don't think Tay truly understood what all that meant until I dropped him off for school one morning. He walked to class, the bell rang, and when he looked up at the doorway I stood there, lunchbox in tow, ready to work.

I saw two smile-filled faces from Tay and his teacher that morning. A new trend started that day.

Chapter 11

Mom Goes Back to Grade School

At this school, as Tay's aide, my interaction with my son was not limited at all. I could hold his hand, walk him out of class, or whisper in his ear to redirect him if necessary. As I spent more time with Tay, his meltdowns diminished. His teacher expressed her happiness about my presence and attributed some of his progress to me. I told her about my positive incentives.

I frequented the local 99 Cents store for items I knew Tay liked and let him dig in a special prize bag for the toys. On days when he was able to settle down in class, he got a prize. I also applied another technique that I couldn't share with the teacher: I leaned into his ear and whispered a threat to tell his father. Hey, the guy's over six feet tall and quietly intimidating. I used what I had. More importantly, Tay liked impressing his father. Kids generally know Mom's on their side, I think, so oftentimes they have a desire to win over their fathers.

What I liked most about this time was our walks outside of class. Once Taylor was having a difficult time with a math worksheet, and we were able to sit outside on a nearby bench to finish. We talked and I connected with my son about why he found the work challenging. Talking through things seemed to work best for him. That's not something a teacher can easily do when she has thirty other students to manage.

I discovered that first grade was nothing like I remembered it. After so many education initiatives that changed the way elementary classrooms worked, I hardly recognized this new era of school.

Most schools in our district couldn't afford full-time physical education instructors anymore. At my son's school, gym was combined with the lunch period. For children with ADHD, movement is essential to their learning. I think removing gym must make school especially harder for these students.

As I'd quit my job to "work" for my son, I was available to assist with homework and in-classroom work as I'd promised. When I sat with him in class, I quickly saw just how much a lack of movement affected children like Tay. He required more breaks than a boxer fighting someone out of his league. I did what I could by giving him squeeze toys and having him do a few jumping jacks outside of class. We had fun together every day.

Then one morning the teacher approached me to let me know I needed to pull back. She wanted me to be less an aide to Tay and more of an assistant to her. She didn't want Tay to be dependent on me, especially since he'd eventually have an appointed aide (who was not his mom). I capitulated.

So I worked with the first-grade children on art projects and tested them in reading comprehension. I also volunteered on various school committees and received early notification on supply needs so I could contribute on a regular basis. I appreciated the immediate feedback and constant communication. I also liked that the teacher's style was calm and methodical, similar to my husband's. I related to her and so did Tay.

By the end of the year, my son's teacher told me she genuinely liked Tay, she'd actually begun to understand him, and she found him funny and creative. I also found out, while I continued as her aide, that I would not need to help him at all in the classroom. His district-appointed aide, stipulated by the IEP, had been hired.

***

Tay's first aide was a man. I thought this was a perfect match, based on gender, but I was wrong. Tay always has to adjust to transitions, and new people count as one of them. He and Tay just didn't get along very well. I tried to assist, but the teacher suggested to me that I pull back. She thought my involvement was impeding the development of my son's relationship with his aide.

However, the district (and it may have even been at the request of the aide) placed someone else in the class for my son. Perhaps they realized the first aide was getting nowhere with Tay. And it actually took two more aides before we found the right match: a composed, athletic woman, undaunted by any of my son's behaviors.

Struggling to contain his impulses, Tay once licked his new aide's arm. A genius at redirection and communicating immediate consequences, she made sure it never happened again. She also knew how to incentivize. She provided really cool squeeze toys he could use when he needed to do something impulsive. Children with ADHD tend to have a difficult time containing impulses, but giving them something to focus on in a controlled way helps.

His new aide's handling of my son was masterful. She even invited him to hang out with her and her niece on school holidays. It was a great match, and I felt relieved. It would be a little sad (okay—who am I kidding—not really), but I'd soon be graduating from first grade. Tay was in capable, loving hands.

***

By the end of my son's first year at the magnet school, he had a team of people working on his behalf, including a resource specialist, a psychologist, a behaviorist, and his beloved classroom aide. While I'd spoken, at least briefly, to everyone who worked with him, I hadn't had a formal meeting in weeks. I looked forward to finding out what they had to say about my first-grader.

Though prepared to make financial adjustments as required, I needed to return to work (at least that's what I'd been told by the boss, aka my husband). So I prayed there was enough progress from the school's perspective. Besides going back to work, I also needed to pull back to spend more time with my other child.

Many times, siblings of children with special needs don't get their share of parental time. This can lead to acting out, or to self-esteem issues. I didn't want that to be the case with my daughter. I'd already started thinking of special things we could do together, such as finger painting and bubble play. We needed time for just the two of us.

When I entered the school office on our next meeting day, I found a large group of people there—including my son's teacher and a couple advisors from our school district. We discussed objectives and progress, and each person reported on Tay's growth. I became more and more emotional. It was at that very moment that I just knew I was starting full-on menopause right in front of these people.

Everyone had something positive to say about where Tay was and had unwavering faith about where he was going. His most difficult tasks, reading and writing, were moving in the right direction. He no longer cried when asked to complete one sentence with correct punctuation on the page. He was asking for library time in order to check out books of interest. He did well in computer lab and started to make friends, instead of being isolated on the playground or at lunch time. His social skills had improved immensely.

He was able to wait his turn when playing with friends and had gotten better about looking directly at people when they spoke to him. He also was able to use words to express his frustration with people, rather than running off. His teacher even beamed when she talked about him and praised his humor and storytelling. She said she planned to give him an opportunity to perform his comedy in front of the class (I should have asked if I could open for him.)

The team unanimously decided that Tay still needed support services in order to be successful. The district would continue to provide them. He was by no means the model student, but he was leagues ahead of where he started and the school year wasn't quite over. More chances for him to grow lay ahead.

Tay's therapist had been right. In a better environment, Tay could thrive. Though it might take years for him to get where he needed to be, he'd get there eventually. Finally, I felt that way. Tears welled in my eyes and I tried to cover my embarrassment with a completely out-of-context joke. But his team understood. A few of them were parents too. They knew their words had lifted a heavy weight from my tired—so tired—shoulders.

When I left the office and hopped into my vehicle, I immediately dialed my husband. He asked if I needed him to be there the next time. I told him it was always great to have him there, but it hadn't been difficult. This meeting was a triumphant one, and I was crying because of the sense of peace I felt over what looked to be a complete turnaround in my son.

I was going to be able to return to work without a flood of phone calls from school and without guilt. Tay had people. He had a support staff. And they liked him. They really liked him.

Chapter 12

The World According to Taylor

I love the Internet. But sometimes it gets me into trouble. After I questioned my OBGYN's decisions about my daughter's birth plan, he asked if I wanted the Internet to deliver the baby for me. When Tay was officially diagnosed with ADHD, I began scouring the Internet for magic cures. I found none. So I had to go in a different direction.

One of the ways my husband and I decided to help Tay was to step into his world of scientific make-believe, where families lived in outer space. Tay loved to imagine that everyone lived in the cosmos, and nothing cost money. He thought that in deep space, we all lived communally and traveled among the planets peacefully. We also moved quickly and survived off candy and pizza. Poverty, war, and hatred did not exist in outer space. Obviously, my NPR listening had gotten to him. He worried incessantly about such things.

The idea of stepping into Tay's world came from a parenting class I took. Supposedly, playing in his world would start to rebuild his self-confidence. Rather than press him into conforming, we'd have to learn to step back and allow him to be himself once in a while. We'd have to let him take the lead.

We tested my theory during a recent Christmas gathering, I asked that the family not correct every single infraction Tay committed. I wanted him to enjoy one day in which he could feel free to be who he was. It isn't often most adults have this pleasure, and certainly in childhood a kid should enjoy it.

So even though Tay stumbled on his feet because he never watched where he was going or he knocked over a dish or two, we didn't reprimand him. He played with his toys until falling into a much-needed sleep. And we all lived.

The more we stepped into Tay's realm, the more we began to understand his point of view. One evening he shared, "sometimes you give me too many things to do at once and I can't remember them all."

He also told me doing homework with a tutor worked better than doing it with the other students in the afterschool program. The afterschool counselors didn't have time to explain things to him that he couldn't remember in class. So I hired a new tutor for him.

Just as Taylor and I developed a collaborative alliance with his educators, I wanted to have the same sort of relationship with him outside of school. I knew, outside of his new school, people didn't look at my son as a child with a learning difference. They looked at him as kid who behaved badly. And if I didn't start to help him develop a toolbox for his hyperactivity, anxiety, memory disorder, sensory processing, and impulse control (all things he struggled with as part of his ADHD), he'd always be dependent upon me.

There were definite parameters and non-negotiables in this process. He had to learn to make eye contact and wait his turn to speak as a gesture of respect. (We're still working on these.). However, if he wanted to repurpose a shipping box for a racetrack or needed to run up and down the block before starting a hard math assignment, I was flexible. And so was Dad.

I wanted him to feel empowered. He had to participate in his own support process. He had to help build the toolbox because he would be using the tools. Most important, Tay had the most at stake if we were wrong.

***

My son's behaviorist at school said she worked with him on a behavior chart. Unlike previous iterations, it broke up his day into chunks and he was rewarded with a happy face when he adhered to classroom rules. After each chunk of time, he was allotted a moment to regroup and return to task.

He set his own goal. One hundred percent focus all day. He even selected an incentive he believed would provide the motivation he needed to meet his objective.

When I picked him up from school toward the end of the school year, he said, "I'm a little upset at my choice earlier."

I asked him what had happened. He told me he'd had to go under his table to sit. When I asked him why he said, "Well Mom, I was acting like a maniac."

We discussed some possible options that might be more appropriate if he felt that way again. His face lit up as he shouted out solutions: "Get my aide!" "Breathe!" "Count to ten!"

I let him come to these answers on his own with encouraging high-fives and smiles. His somber attitude transformed into a triumphant one and he began to look forward to the next day, when he could utilize his strategies if needed. Our short conversation took little effort. But at the end of it, he felt successful and so did I.

In other words, he used careful reflection to resolve his actions on his own. That was huge.

Weeks later, my redheaded, freckled kid with almond skin beamed when I picked him up from school. He shoved a piece of paper in my face and announced with operatic vibrato, "Read this!"

Tay's behavior chart had a score of one hundred percent. We high-fived, chest-bumped, fist-bumped, and laughed.

When we arrived at our house, I told Tay he deserved a reward. Of course he agreed. The kid lives for incentives. I assured him he deserved a model car as promised. But such a win warranted two prizes. I pulled down the prize bag that I kept hidden in my home office and retrieved a book. It didn't receive as much fanfare as the model car, but he seemed to take an interest in it.

Then it happened. I mean the truly remarkable … happened.

My son walked to the dining room, sat down at the table, and began to read. No tears, no falls to the floor, no screams, just reading. He even sounded out words he didn't recognize without prompting. He asked for help when he got stumped. Nothing like it had taken place pretty much since kindergarten.

Just weeks before, reading had been an arduous task that turned the whole household upside down. Language arts would go something like this:

"How many words?"
"How long?"
"How many sentences?"

Then the tears, the flailing, the falling out of the chair, the wind of exhaustion pushing through his father's voice, my need to leave the room, and the spirit of complete loss. An assignment that should've taken ten minutes turned into sixty or more. Nothing seemed to work—not the behavior charts I created with pictures and stickers, not the incentives we utilized for other tasks, not even letting Tay run beforehand had seemed to affect this one area of homework as much as we desired.

But in that moment, I realized something had worked. We just hadn't understood it—one of the things that confirmed Tay's genius.

I noticed Tay achieved this day's milestone with a tool. On our table sat a short stack of plastic, basket-weaved placemats. While Tay read, he moved his fingers across the mats. He also leaned back and forth in his seat. Behavior that had earned him penalties earlier in his education, actually supported him. The adults didn't understand he knew what he was doing all along.

Tay reached the end of the book and closed it with a pleased grin. Fighting back tears, I leaned in to hug my son and congratulated him on his success. He said the kind of thing he is inclined to say these days.

"Yeah, I'm smart."

Epilogue

With the last chapter of this book, I feel as though I'm also closing a chapter of my life. But I know it's also just the beginning. We've said goodbye to some of the old challenges, such as Tay's lengthy tantrums during language-arts lessons. And we're attending to growing needs, such as bonding with children to create friendships and fully comprehending the impediments inherent in his disability.

"One day I will make a school for boys of color who have learning disabilities," Tay recently said. He recognizes the unique challenge of teaching boys who have distinctive learning and cultural needs. Who better than my son to support boys like him one day?

Unfortunately, I'm still working through the aftermath of Tay's first year of school. It occasionally comes up when he's learning new material or contemplating how challenging the curriculum will be in the next grade. He's capable of more than he realizes. We need to build his confidence and assure him that when adults don't understand him, it's not his fault. We have to manage his anxiety each new school year. Each grade he enters means a new teacher, new classmates, new routines. His one-to-one aide is in place to mitigate any unease. But it's not a perfect science. And he will be losing his familiar aide again soon as she relocates to another city.

Since that first year of school, Tay has seen a neurologist who diagnosed him with epilepsy. He often stared for long periods of time, and some of the school staff assumed the symptoms stemmed from ADHD. However, a thorough evaluation proved otherwise. The epilepsy is managed with medication, significantly reducing his seizures.

Taylor also received an Autism Spectrum Disorder (ASD) diagnosis. ASD is a term for a spectrum closely related disorder with a shared core of symptoms. Each person on the spectrum has difficulty with social interaction, empathy, communication and flexible behavior (though the extent of these behaviors varies widely). According to the Centers for Disease Control and Prevention, approximately 1 in 68 US children are identified as having ASD. Tay has a lot of support in place to assure his strengths are enhanced.

Tay's music therapy continues. The class, which takes place at a local college, is private. The goals are to promote emotional and creative expression, encourage tension release, and increase focus. His instructor uses a variety of instruments such as the piano and the kalimbas, African thumb pianos. Tay has participated in lengthy musical improvisations between the kalimba and the piano. He also uses drums to release pent-up tension. His teacher validates Tay by recognizing his musical accomplishments, and she plays with him to demonstrate she values his ideas and opinions. Recently, he played some of the melody of Lukas Graham's "7 Years," a current favorite, on the piano.

We increased his hours of therapy at school and placed him in a therapeutic swimming and therapeutic art program.

Each new year and environment presents a new adventure. In many school districts, the entire administrative staff might change due to reorganization, budget cuts, or administrators leaving the profession altogether. So for Tay, a great deal of emotional preparation takes place over the summer. We highlight the fun of meeting new classmates and learning new things. We talk ad nauseam about the fortunate parts of starting a new phase of learning. It takes him a long time to buy into it, and that can be draining.

Yet I'd be remiss if I didn't acknowledge how truly blessed we are. There's a strong support crew in our circle. Among our Tay fan club members are the staff at Tay's school, private professionals, family, and cherished friends. I've learned the value of them all.

I've also come away with these important life lessons to guide me in the years going forward:

Gratitude

Daily gratitude is among the most important parts of healing. Beginning each day with gratitude sets the tone for what lies ahead. Sometimes the sheer fatigue of being a parent doesn't allow for extensive meditation. Any amount will do. The important thing is that it gets done regularly.

Forgiveness

Getting it wrong does not mean all is lost. I have and will continue to get things wrong. But I cannot stay stuck in that place. The only way to figure out the next step is to stop dwelling on the previous one. Forgiveness of anyone who has harmed you and forgiveness of yourself is an essential part of healing.

Acceptance

Children tell grownups what they need, but it's up to the grownups to listen. I have learned to accept our son for who he is. I have learned to hear him. He may not always have the appropriate words. But he is constantly communicating.

Strength

We innately know more and have more strength than we think. When trials present themselves to us as parents, we will conquer them. All of them. This is a truth we must know.

***

I am hopeful about seeing even more shifts in Tay's life through love, encouragement, and prayer. I do not expect the progress to be swift. And there's a high probability that my recurring dream—the one where I'm standing on that window ledge—will not fade away completely until Tay graduates from college.

In the meantime, I discover, I shift, I make mistakes (like forgetting a lunch or taking a circuitous new route somewhere that sends Tay to level-ten freak-out status). In the midst of my own mistakes, I try to acknowledge Tay's success. It looks different for him than it might look for another child. For example, sitting through a church service (with his ears covered to muffle the sound) deserves a huge accolade.

Tay is truly exceptional, and each day my husband I are challenged with bringing him to that awareness as well. Though we have struggled both as individuals and as a unit, the two of us have matured as people because of Tay. For that alone, I am grateful. In the end, we know we will get through it.

Nine-year-old Tay says it best: "I really am a genius. It's just difficult to see it sometimes."

Resources

IEP Meeting: Quick Tips

Before the Meeting

- Don't be afraid to have a good cry before your meeting if you need to (Also keep tissues on-hand during the meeting and don't wear your favorite mascara.)
- Invest in a nice stress aid.
- Include your significant other or close friend in the process.
- If you have vacation time, take the day off so you're not rushed or stressed if your appointment goes long.
- Print out-of-the box accommodations you believe might be helpful for your particular child; they probably won't have those things in the meeting (Look online for apps, tools, new technology.)
- If you have time, keep a journal of your child's work habits and behavior around schoolwork and bring it to your child's IEP meeting.
- Schedule a facial or massage (or both) for immediately following your IEP meeting.
- Find a local support group for parents whose children have similar learning challenges and who share IEP experiences.
- Develop a village of friends who can provide support through the process.
- Bring reading material in case your team is running late.
- Listen to your favorite song on the way in (get pumped up for victory).
- Sing loudly in your car (it's therapeutic).
- Attend a local IEP workshop.
- Don't fight with anyone the morning of your IEP meeting.
- Look at your child and think about how great he or she is.
- Eat your favorite food for breakfast.
- Pick up treats for everyone to share because it disarms people (and makes you happy).

- If you're into caffeine, have coffee or tea (You need to be alert.)
- Pray or meditate.

During the Meeting

- If you feel like you'll need backup, bring an advocate for support (This can be a friend, family member, or professional advocate.)
- Have your reading glasses (if you wear them).
- Don't be afraid to ask questions if you don't understand something.
- Take deep, affirming breaths.
- Smile a lot.

After the Meeting

- Give yourself a high-five because you're awesome!
- Forgive yourself.
- Take a warm bath or soak your feet the night of your meeting.
- Play with your kid and have fun the night of your meeting.
- Eat chocolate (dark, white, really doesn't matter).
- Take a long nap following your meeting.
- Enjoy your favorite kid's movie with your child.
- Call your best friend to vent.
- Make an appointment with a therapist.
- Buy yourself something nice you can afford (like a nice lunch or dinner).
- Watch your favorite comedian's TV special.
- Remember how great you are as a parent.
- Let it all go (Remember, you're awesome.)
- Pray or Meditate.

Terms

A

Applied Behavior Analysis (ABA): The application of behavioral principles to increase and decrease behaviors.

Adapted Physical Education (APE): Specially designed physical education program, using accommodations designed to fit the needs of students who require developmental or corrective instruction in PE.

Accommodations: Changes that allow a person with a disability to participate fully in an activity. Examples include extended time, different test format, and alterations to a classroom.

ADD/ADHD: Attention deficit disorder and attention deficit hyperactivity disorder are medical conditions characterized by a child's inability to focus, while possessing impulsivity, fidgeting, and inattention.

Auditory Integration Training: It typically involves twenty half-hour sessions over ten days listening to specially filtered and modulated music. Used in the early 1990s as a treatment for autism, it has been promoted as a treatment for ADHD, depression, and a wide variety of other disorders.

Anxiety in Children: Defined as extreme agitation, filled with tension and dread. Anxiety differs from fear. Children with anxiety may or may not qualify for special education. Those who need modifications to their school day can achieve this via a 504 plan.

Assessment or Evaluation: Term used to describe the testing and diagnostic processes leading up to the development of an appropriate IEP for a student with special education needs.

Assistive Technology and Alternative Communication (ATAC): Equipment or product system, whether acquired commercially off the shelf, modified, or customized, that is used to increase, maintain, or improve the functional capabilities of a child with a disability.

Asperger Syndrome: A type of pervasive developmental disorder (PDD) that involves delays in the development of basic skills, including socializing, coordination, and the ability to communicate.

Autism: A brain development disorder characterized by impaired social interaction, communication, and restricted and repetitive behavior. Signs usually begin before a child is three years old.

B

Behavior Intervention Plan (BIP): Special education term that describes the written plan used to address problem behavior that includes positive behavioral interventions, strategies, and support. May include program modifications and supplementary aids and services.

Bipolar Disorders: Characterized by cycles of mania alternating with depression. It is difficult to diagnose children with this disorder and often controversial.

Blindness: Condition defined by lacking visual perception due to physiological or neurological factors.

C

Cerebral Palsy (CP): A series of motor problems and physical disorders related to brain injury. CP causes uncontrollable reflex movements and muscle tightness and may cause problems in balance and depth perception. Severe cases can result in mental retardation, seizures, or vision and hearing problems.

Children with Special Needs: A forum that provides resources and community for families with special needs children. www.childrenwithspecialneeds.com

Community Advisory Committee (CAC): A committee whose membership includes parents of school children, school personnel, and representatives of the public. This committee advises school administration and local school boards regarding the plan for special education, assists with parent education, and promotes public awareness of individuals with special needs.

Complaint Procedure: A formal complaint filed with the County or State Board of Education if a district violates a legal duty or fails to follow a requirement under the Individuals with Disabilities Education Act. (IDEA)

Cumulative File: The records maintained by the local school district for any child enrolled in school. The file may contain evaluations and information about a child's disability and placement. It also contains grades and the results of standardized assessments. Parents have the right to inspect these files at any time.

D

Deafness: Hearing impairment so severe that a child is impaired in possessing any linguistic information through hearing.

Designated Instruction Services (DIS): Instruction and services not normally provided by regular classes, resource specialist programs, or special day classes. They include speech therapy and adaptive physical education.

Differential Standards for Graduation: Standards for graduation that may be modified for students with exceptional needs.

Disability: Physical or mental impairment that substantially limits one or more major life activities.

Due Process: Special education term used to describe the process where parents may disagree with the program recommendations of the school district. The notice must be given in writing within thirty days. IDEA provides two methods for resolving disputes: mediation or fair hearing.

E

Early Intervention: Programs for developmentally delayed infants and toddlers through thirty-five months of age; designed to help prevent problems as the child matures.

Emotional Disturbance (SED): Term used to describe a diagnosable mental, behavioral, or emotional disorder that lasts for a significant duration and that meets the criteria within the Diagnostic and Statistical Manual of Mental Disorders.

Extended School Year Services (ESY): An extended school year is a component of special education services for students with unique needs who require services in excess of the regular academic year. Extended year often refers to summer school.

F

Free Appropriate Public Education (FAPE): Special education and related services are provided at public expense, without charge to the parents.

Functional Behavioral Assessment (FBA): A problem-solving process for addressing inappropriate behavior.

H

Hearing Impairment: Full or partial decrease in the ability to detect or understand sounds.

Home/Hospital Instruction: Students with verified medical conditions, which prevent them from attending school, may receive services on a temporary basis in the home or hospital with a physician's referral.

I

Inclusion: Term used to describe services that place students with disabilities in general education classrooms with appropriate support services. Student may receive instruction from both a general education teacher and a special education teacher.

Individuals with Disabilities Education Act (IDEA 2004): The original legislation was written in 1975 guaranteeing students with disabilities a free and appropriate public education and the right to be educated with their non-disabled peers. Congress has reauthorized this federal law. The most recent revision occurred in 2004.

Individualized Education Plan (IEP): Special education term outlined by IDEA to define the written document that states the disabled child's goals, objectives, and services for students receiving special education.

Independent Educational Evaluation (IEE): A school district is required by law to conduct assessments for students who may be eligible for special education. If the parent disagrees with the results of a school district's evaluation conducted on their child, they have the right to request an independent educational evaluation. The district must provide parents with information about how to obtain an IEE. An independent educational evaluation means an evaluation conducted by a qualified examiner who is not employed by the school district. Public expense means the school district pays for the full cost of the evaluation and that it is provided at no cost to the parent.

Individualized Education Program Team: Term used to describe the committee of parents, teachers, administrators, and school personnel that provides services to the student. The committee may also include medical professionals and other relevant parties. The team reviews assessment results, and determines goals, objectives, and program placement for the child needing services.

Individualized Family Service Plan (IFSP): A process of providing early intervention services for children ages zero through three with special needs. Family-based needs are identified and a written plan is developed and reviewed periodically.

Individualized Transition Plan (ITP): This plan starts at age fourteen and addresses areas of post-school activities, post-secondary education, employment, community experiences, and daily living skills.

L

Least Restrictive Environment (LRE): The placement of a special-needs student in a manner promoting the maximum possible interaction with the general school population. Placement options are offered on a continuum including regular classroom with no support services, regular classroom with support services, designated instruction services, special day classes, and private special education programs.

Local Education Agency (LEA): Term used to describe a school district participating in a SELPA (*Special Education Local Plan Area*).

Local Plan: A plan developed by a SELPA and submitted to the State Department of Education for approval. The document outlines the plan for delivery of support services to eligible students living within the geographic boundaries of the plan.

M

Mainstreaming: Term used to describe the integration of children with special needs into regular classrooms for part of the school day. The remainder of the day is in a special education classroom.

Manifestation Determination: Within ten school days of any decision to change the placement of a child with a disability because of violation of school code, the IEP team must review all relevant information in the student's file to determine if the conduct in question was caused by the child's disability or if the conduct was a direct result of the school district's failure to implement the child's IEP.

Mental Retardation (now referred to as Intellectually Disabled): This term has recently been changed. This disorder is characterized by below-average cognitive functioning in two or more adaptive behaviors with onset before age eighteen.

Multiple Disabilities: An IEP term used to define a combination of disabilities that causes severe educational needs requiring multiple special education programs such as mental retardation with blindness.

N

Non-public School (NPS): Districts contract with non-public schools when an appropriate placement cannot be found within the scope of the public education setting. Non-public school placement is sought only after efforts to find appropriate placement in public schools have been exhausted.

O

Obsessive-Compulsive Disorder (OCD): OCD is an anxiety disorder that presents itself as recurrent, persistent obsessions or compulsions. Obsessions are intrusive ideas, thoughts, or images while compulsions are repetitive behaviors or mental acts that the child feels he or she must perform.

Occupational Therapists: Provide consultation and support to staff to improve a student's educational performance related to fine-motor, gross-motor, and sensory-integration development.

Oppositional Defiant Disorder (ODD): A child who defies authority by disobeying, talking back, arguing or being hostile in a way that is excessive compared to other children, and this pattern continues for more than six months, may be determined to have ODD. ODD often occurs with other behavioral problems such as ADHD, learning disabilities, and anxiety disorders.

Orthopedic Impairment: Term used to define impairments caused by congenital anomaly, impairments by diseases, and impairments by other causes.

Other Health Impaired: Term used to describe limited strength, vitality, and alertness that results in limited ability in the educational environment. Impairment could be the result of chronic health problems such as asthma, attention deficit disorder, heart condition, hemophilia, leukemia, nephritis, rheumatic fever, and sickle cell anemia.

P

Parent Consent: Special education term used by IDEA that states you have been fully informed in your native language or other mode of communication of all the information about the action for which you are giving consent and that you understand and agree in writing to that action.

Physical Therapists: Provide consultation and support to staff to improve a student's educational performance related to functional gross-motor development.

Private School: There are new laws regulating the rights of students with disabilities whose parents place them in private schools. When a student is enrolled in private school and has academic difficulties, the school where the student attends needs to inform the parent and the local public school district of the student's difficulties. The district of residence may assess the student to determine if the student qualifies for special education. If he or she does qualify, the district of residence is responsible for writing an Individualized Education Plan.

R

Residential and Private Placements: Part B of IDEA does not require a school district to pay for the cost of education for your disabled child at a private school or facility if the school district made free appropriate public education available to your child and you chose to place your child in private placement.

Resource Specialists: Provide instructional planning and support and direct services to students whose needs have been identified in an IEP and are assigned to general education classrooms for the majority of their school day.

Resource Specialist Program (RSP): Term used to describe a program that provides instruction, materials, and support services to students with identified disabilities who are assigned to general classrooms for more than fifty percent of their school day.

S

School Psychologist: Assist in the identification of intellectual, social, and emotional needs of students. They provide consultation and support to families and staff regarding behavior and conditions related to learning. They plan programs to meet the special needs of children and often serve as a facilitator during an IEP meeting.

Sensory Processing Disorder: A complex brain disorder that causes a child to misinterpret everyday sensory information like movement, sound, and touch. Children with SPD may seek out intense sensory experiences or feel overwhelmed with information.

Specific Learning Disability: Special education term used to define a disorder in one or more of the basic psychological processes involved in understanding or using language spoken or written that may manifest itself in an imperfect ability to listen, think, speak, read, write, spell, or perform mathematical equations.

Speech and Language Impairments: Communication disorders such as stuttering, impaired articulation, language impairment, or voice impairment.

Speech and Language Specialists: Assess students for possible delayed speech and language skills and provide direct services in the area of phonology, morphology, syntax, semantics and pragmatics. They are also available regarding hearing impairments and amplification.

SSDI: Social security disability insurance benefits are provided to qualified individuals who cannot engage in substantial gainful work activity because of a disability and who have paid into the system or have a parent who has paid into the Social Security system.

SSI: Supplemental Security Income benefits are provided to qualified individuals who cannot engage in substantial gainful work activity because of a disability and who fall below certain assets and income levels.

Special Day Class (SDC): Term used to describe a self-contained special education class which provides services to students with intensive needs that cannot be met by the general education program, RSP, or DIS program. Classes consist of more than fifty percent of the student's day.

State Schools: Most states operate state-run residential schools for deaf and blind students.

Student Study Team (SST): A group that evaluates a child's performance, makes recommendations for success, and develops a formal plan. The team includes the classroom teacher, parents, and educational specialists. They may make a recommendation for a special education evaluation.

T

Tourette Syndrome: Disorder that includes multiple motor and one or more vocal tics, which occur many times per day, nearly daily. If a child has Tourette's syndrome, symptoms tend to appear between the ages of three and ten years old.

Traumatic Brain Injury: An acquired injury to the brain caused by an external physical force resulting in total or partial functional disability or psychosocial impairment. Applies to open- or closed-head injuries.

Transition IEP: IDEA mandates that at age sixteen, the IEP must include a statement about transition, including goals for post-secondary activities and the services needed to achieve these goals. This is referred to as an Individual Transition Plan or (ITP).

Turner's Syndrome: This rare genetic disorder affects females and is characterized by the absence of an X chromosome. Characteristics include small stature, limited development of sexual characteristics, low hairline, and abnormal eye and bone development.

V

Visual Impairment: Impairment in vision that even with correction adversely affects a child's educational performance.

Vision Specialists: Provide consultation and support to staff and direct instructional support to students with visual impairments. They provide functional vision assessments and curriculum modifications including Braille, large type, and aural media.

W

Workability Program: These programs focus on preparing high school students with disabilities for successful transition to employment, continuing education, and quality adult life with an emphasis on work-based learning opportunities.

Tools

School Checklist

When evaluating a school for your child, it's useful to have a checklist handy in order to measure how the school fits your particular needs. The following is a general checklist you can utilize as a guide.

Checklist

- What is the student-to-teacher ratio?
- What training does the staff have on your child's particular learning difference?
- What post-graduation support do they offer?
- Is the school accredited or licensed by the state? Accreditation and licensing means there is oversight.
- What are the day-to-day activities?
- Is there continued learning for the staff in the area of special needs? If so, what does it entail?
- Are the stimuli you observe something that your child can handle? Is the classroom noise level too loud? Are the walls too visually cluttered with student projects?
- How do they deal with behavior issues in the classroom?
- Do they use any adaptive technology?
- How do they evaluate students?
- Are counseling services part of their program?
- What is the climate on parent involvement? Do they have strong parent support groups on campus? Do parents have oversight on any policies or procedures?
- How much access will you have to your child's classroom for observance?

Sample To-Do Lists

Before School

- Wash your face
- Brush your teeth
- Put on sunscreen
- Put on your clothes
- Empty the small wastebaskets
- Wash your hands
- Eat your breakfast
- Get your backpack
- Put your lunch in your backpack
- Wait for your parents at the front door
- HAVE AN AMAZING DAY!

After School

- Check the mailbox
- Bring the mail into the house
- Place your backpack on the table
- Remove important papers from your backpack
- Give important papers to a parent or grandparent
- Remove homework from your backpack
- Ask an adult for help
- BE AWESOME!

***Bedtime each night is 8:00 PM
***Media is Friday – Sunday

Tay earns "chips" for completing his tasks that he can use to earn media time, stickers and other fun things.

Love Notes To A Child

Notes that you can cut out and use to put in your child's lunch box to lift his/her spirits. It's one way to reinforce that learning differences do not make a difference in the way you see your child. Download yours at: www.myiepjourney.com

Assessment Letter 3 Be's

I suggest the following be included in any initial request for an IEP assessment, as well as any subsequent request if your first request denied:

Be Specific

State the relevant behaviors of your child that are causing you concern. Some people are afraid to be specific in writing because they don't want their child(ren) to be labeled. If your child is falling behind due to a learning disability, he or she is already labeled. Your observations just provide the context needed to get your child appropriate services. The letter starts a timeline and provides a necessary paper trail. This could be the first step in changing things for your child.

Be Knowledgeable

Look up the Special Education Law for your state and use that language in the request. This shows the administration that you have done your homework and you are serious. In districts where the budget is weak, the first response might be to deny your child his or her right to assessments. Adding the legal language communicates to the administration that you are aware of your rights as a parent.

Be A Team Player

Use language that shows you are collaborative and want to help the school educate your child. You do not need to come in prepared for a battle unless your initial request is denied (in that case, it's "game on" as it relates to working on your child's behalf). Communicate your willingness to support your child in any way necessary. But be honest with both the staff and yourself. If you cannot go off and quit your job in order to be in the classroom (like the extreme choice I made), don't offer that level of support. Offer what you are able to provide and don't feel guilty about the demands of your job or other obligations in your life. The job of the school staff is to educate our children, and our job is to provide a clean, safe home for our children. We know what it takes to accomplish that.

Communicating with Officials

The following is a sample of an IEP letter:

Dear {School Administrator}:

I am the parent [or legal guardian] of [full name of student and date of birth]. This letter is a formal request for an evaluation to determine his/her eligibility for special education provisions. I have been concerned that he/she is not progressing at a proper pace in school and that he/she may need some specialized support in order to receive a fair and appropriate education. I am requesting that an IEP meeting be held for [full name of student] as soon as possible, and in no more than 30 days after the date of the letter, as required by law.

My reasons for requesting the evaluation are [list one or two concerns you have observed about your child's learning].

It is my goal to have a collaborative relationship with the school and I am willing to meet with you in advance of any assessments in order to share information that might be helpful about [full name of student]. I am available on the following days and times: [list a few options for meeting with school staff].

Please contact me about next steps in the evaluation process.

Sincerely,

[Parent/Guardian name and the date]

The following is a sample of a post IEP letter:

Dear {School Administrator}:

Thank you for taking the time to meet with me to discuss [name of child]'s needs in the classroom. I am looking forward to a collaborative relationship. After conducting research about support that might be helpful for my child, I have the following suggestions [list a few suggestions that are applicable to your child]:

Suggestion 1
Suggestion 2
Suggestion 3

I would like to discuss a realistic implementation timeline with the IEP team. I am available on the following dates and times: (list a few options for meeting with school staff or having a conference call)

I look forward to meeting again soon.

Sincerely,

[Parent/Guardian Name & the Date]

It is important that all correspondence between you and the school staff is documented, even if it's via email.

√ IEP Checklist

The following is a checklist you can use to determine if your IEP has all of the elements you need:

- Are there annual goals and are they clearly stated?
- Are the goals measurable?
- Do the goals appear to relate to your child's needs?
- Does the IEP specify how the goals can be obtained?
- Has the school provided evidence that the services they offer have been effective with other children who have those same special needs?
- Do you understand the information in your child's present level of performance (PLOP) section, and is it supported with evaluation data from standardized testing or state or district assessments?
- Does the PLOP section provide information about your child's developmental, academic, and functional needs?
- Does the IEP state the amount of days/times/length of time your child will be pulled out of class for services? If so, is it satisfactory to you?
- Does the IEP identify the staff who will be responsible for implementing your child's services?
- Based on what YOU know about your child, do the services offered seem appropriate?
- Does the IEP document show how information will be distributed among the school staff?
- Does the IEP explain whether or not your child will participate in state and/or district testing?
- Have all of your requested accommodations been included?
- Have any negative consequences of special education been explained to you, such as your child's inability to progress to the next grade? (Note: In some states, this is not allowed.)

If at any point you believe it is necessary to have an advocate in your IEP meeting, please seek someone so that you feel confident and secure. Your school should support the presence of a professional or a knowledgeable friend or family member if that is your request. Most importantly, if you do not agree with the IEP, do not sign it. This is a document for your child and should reflect what the entire team believes is best for the student.

Helpful Websites

Though some of the below websites refer to regional resources (in California), they might provide ideas for your search in your area.

22 Mobile Apps
Rosenberg, Julie Z. (May, 2012) "22 Mobile Apps for Children with Learning Differences." Care.com, www.care.com/c/stories/6621/22-best-mobile-apps-for-kids-with-special-needs.

Additude Magazine
An online periodical that provides strategies and support for people who have ADHD and their families. www.additudemag.com

Advocating Change Together (ACT)
ACT is operated by and for individuals with developmental disorders or other disabilities. www.selfadvocacy.org/contact/

A Parent's Guide to Autism Spectrum Disorder
A comprehensive and informative site provided by the National Institute of Mental Health. The site offers a wide array of knowledge regarding symptoms, resources and opportunities to connect with organizations nationwide. www.nimh.nih.gov/health/publications/autism-spectrum-disorder-qf-15-5511/index.shtml

The Association for Persons with Severe Handicaps (TASH)
TASH is an international group for people with disabilities, their families and advocates, aiming for the inclusion of special needs individuals in all aspects of society. www.tash.org

Autism Society of America
Autism has steadily inclined in numbers. This group encourages lifelong access and opportunities for children with autism or Asperger syndrome, as well as their families. www.autism-society.org

Autism Speaks
The world's leading autism science and advocacy organization, dedi-

cated to funding research into the causes, prevention, treatments and a cure for autism; increasing awareness of autism spectrum disorders; and advocating for the needs of individuals with autism and their families. They have an extensive web community where parents can share, connect, discuss and support each other through their autism journey. www.autismspeaks.org

Benefits for Children with Disabilities
https://www.ssa.gov/pubs/EN-05-10026.pdf. Washington, DC.

California Department of Education
An educational resource site for the state of California. www.cde.ca.gov

Children's Disabilities
Created by a parent of a special needs child to provide help and resources in the form of articles, books etc. regarding a vast spectrum of topics relating to special needs and disabilities. They review other books and articles from authors. www.childrensdisabilities.info

Department of Developmental Services
The main agency that provides help for people with disabilities in CA. Services and supports are provided through a combination of federal, state, county and local government services, private businesses, support groups and volunteers. www.dds.ca.gov/rc

The Disability Network
Provides information on any subject related to living independently with all disabilities. Refers individuals to other agencies in their community to assist in gathering independence. www.disnetwork.org

Education.com
Worksheets, educational games and more! Hutton, Shannon. (2013) "Helping Kinesthetic Learners Succeed." Education.com, www.education.com/magazine/article/kinesthetic_learner.

Family Focus Research Center (CSUN)
Part of the CSUN Michael D. Eisner College of Education. The goal of the Family Focus Resource Center (FFRC) is to empower families to advocate for their children and adults with special needs so they can

receive the most effective services and greatest opportunities resulting in productive, inclusive and enriched lives. www.csun.edu/family-focus-resource-center

Child Development Institute
Free community play and learning space in Canoga Park, CA. www.cdikids.org

Grant Services for Children/Families with Special Needs
www.curedfoundation.org/docs/grant_sources_2011.pdf

Great Schools
A website you can use to find and research local schools in your district. www.greatschools.org

Helpguide.org
A comprehensive resources site brought to you by Helpguide, a non-profit organization aimed at increasing the quality of life for the mentally disabled and their families. www.helpguide.org

I Can Do This, but I Can't Do That (HBO Movie)
A film for families about learning differences. www.hbo.com/documentaries/i-cant-do-this-but-i-can-do-that-a-film-for-families-about-learning-differences/index.html

Kids Like Me - L.A.: Part of The Help Program
Provides fun enrichment programs and after school activities for kids on the spectrum, ages from preschool to high school. www.kidslikemela.org

Learning Disabilities Association of America
A one-stop shop resource for families, professionals, children and educators. This site not only offers webinars and self-help videos, but also provides additional resources in terms of other organizations and groups. Of additional note, this site addresses any and all potential diagnoses for your family member. www.ldaamerica.org

Learning Disability Checklist
A list of some signs of learning and attention issues in adults. Kelly,

Kate. (2014) "Checklist: The Signs of Learning and Attention Issues in Adults." Understood.org, https://www.understood.org/en/family/taking-care-of-yourself/do-i-have-learning-attention-issue/checklist-the-signs-of-learning-and-attention-issues-in-adults

National Alliance for the Mentally Ill (NAMI)
The focus of this organization is to be a support to individuals with mental illness and their families.
www.nami.org; www.nami.org/Find-Support

National Association of Education for Young Children (NAEYC)
This resource offers listings for schools in your area and additional information for families and teachers. http://families.naeyc.org; http://families.naeyc.org/learning-and-development/child-development/parent-teacher-conferences

National Center for Learning Disabilities (NCLD)
An advocacy site for parents, families and children that focuses on everything from day-to-day challenges and triumphs to self-care for the parent. www.ncld.org

Parent Center Hub
Parent Training and Information (PTI) Centers that provide information and resources for families of children with special needs and disabilities throughout the USA. To find a PTI Center in your area: www.parentcenterhub.org/find-your-center

Parent-Child Interaction Therapy (PCIT)
A Parent Training Workshop for conduct-disordered young children that places emphasis on improving the quality of the parent-child relationship and changing parent-child interaction patterns. It is usually conducted with a therapist but self-instructed options are available as well. www.chp.phhp.ufl.edu

Regional Centers
California has 21 regional centers with more than 40 offices located throughout the state that serve individuals with developmental disabilities and their families.
They provide diagnosis and assessment of eligibility and help plan,

access, coordinate and monitor the services and supports. There is no charge for the diagnosis and eligibility assessment. Once eligibility is determined, most services and supports are free regardless of age or income. www.dds.ca.gov/rc/RCList.cfm

Sensory Processing Disorder Treatment Directory
Lists some therapists in the U.S. and elsewhere who are certified to perform the Sensory Integration Praxis Test (SIPT). While you may not want to pay the very high fee for a SIPT evaluation, it may be possible to get treatment from a SIPT-certified therapist. www.spdstar.org

Smart Kids with Learning Disabilities
This website was created to educate, guide and inspire parents of children with learning disabilities. www.smartkidswithld.org/getting-help

Special Ed
Learning disabilities checklists. Prepare for your child's IEP meeting with these checklists. www.specialed.about.com/cs/learningdisabled/a/learningd.-06J.htm

Special Needs Alliance (SNA)
The Special Needs Alliance is a national, not-for-profit organization of attorneys dedicated to the practice of disability and public benefits law. Find a special needs attorney in your area. www.specialneedsalliance.org/find-an-attorney

Special Needs Network (SNN)
The purpose of the Special Needs Network is to raise public awareness of developmental disabilities and to impact public policy while providing education and resources to families, children and adults. SNN serves as a link between under-served communities and mainstream developmental disability organizations and governmental institutions, which often fail to address issues specific to these communities. www.snnla.org

Task California
An advocacy site for individuals with disabilities aimed at enhancing the quality of life for all. While focusing specifically on Southern California, the methodologies and resources can be mirrored to reflect your local

environment. www.taskca.org

Teach-Nology
A website that provides teacher resources, but has a very helpful and extensive list of Special needs and Ed organizations. www.teach-nology. com/teachers/special_ed/organizations

TED Talks
A playlist of 10 videos exploring the science of autism. www.ted.com/ playlists/153/the_autism_spectrum

Triple P
A parenting resource site that provides newsletters, seminars and real-life scenarios with tools and techniques aimed at empowering both the parent and child. www.triplep.net/glo-en/home

U.S. Department of Education
An information page within the U.S. Department of Education, which speaks directly to Section 504 of the Rehabilitation Act. The goal of the discussion here is to discuss FAPE (Free Appropriate Public Education). www2.ed.gov/about/offices/list/ocr/docs/edlite-FAPE504.html

Our city hosts a Special Needs Fair each year with a variety of vendors, one of which provides respite services for parents. Respite service is temporary care of a dependent, providing relief for their usual caregivers. For example, this allows parents to get away in order to have much needed time to themselves. I suggest finding such a program locally, as these sorts of programs often have connections to many agencies that provide a range of resources.

Great Reads

1-2-3 Magic
Phelan, Thomas W. (2016) *1-2-3 Magic: 3-Step Discipline for Calm, Effective, and Happy Parenting* (6th Edition) Illinois: ParentMagic, Inc.

All About IEPs
W. D. Wright, Peter, et al. (2010) Wrightslaw: *All About IEPs*. Virginia: Harbor House Law Press, Inc.

Chicken Soup
www.chickensoup.com

Developing Your Child's Self-Esteem
Lyness, D'Arcy. (2016) Developing Your Child's Self-Esteem. Kidshealth.org, www.kidshealth.org/en/parents/self-esteem.html

LA Parent Magazine (special needs section)
Events and resources for families in Los Angeles with children who have special needs. The site connects families with sources of support and fun. Provides a monthly special needs newsletter. www.laparent.com/content/special-needs

The Motivation Breakthrough
www.ricklavoie.com/motivationbreakthrough.html

Out of Sync Child
Kranowitz, Carol. (2005) *"The Out-of-Sync Child: Recognizing and Coping with Sensory Processing Disorder."* New York: Penguin Group, Inc. www.out-of-sync-child.com

Parenting with Love and Logic
www.loveandlogic.com/parenting-with-love-and-logic

Smart but Scattered Kids
Dawson, Peg and Richard Guare. (2009) "Smart but Scattered: The Revolutionary 'Executive Skills' Approach to Helping Kids Reach Their

Potential." New York: The Guilford Press. www.smartbutscatteredkids. com

The Special EDge Newsletter
A publication of the California Department of Education special education division. www.calstat.org/specialEdge.html

The Trouble with Boys
Tyre, Peg. (2008) "*The Trouble with Boys: A Surprising Report Card on Our Sons, Their Problems at School, and What Parents and Educators Must Do.*" New York: Three Rivers Press. www.pegtyre.com/trouble.php

Twice-Exceptional Newsletter
A newsletter that provides resources for parents of children who are gifted with learning differences. Bracamonte, Micaela. (2010) "*Twice-exceptional Students: Who Are They and What Do They Need?*" http://www.2enewsletter.com/article_2e_what_are_they.html

Women's Comfort Series
Louden, Jennifer. (2005) "*The Woman's Comfort Book: A Self-Nurturing Guide for Restoring Balance in Your Life.*" New York: HarperOne. www.jenniferlouden.com/products/books

More Resources for Parents

A Guide on Due Process
CADRE (2014). "IDEA Special Education Due Process Complaints/ Hearing Requests Including Expedited Hearing Requests," Eugene, Oregon, CADRE. www.directionservice.org/cadre/pdf/DueProcessParent-Guide_2014.pdf

Public Counsel, a Pro Bono Law Firm
610 South Ardmore Avenue
Los Angeles, CA 90005
Local: (213) 385-2977
Fax: (213) 385-9089
Website: www.publiccounsel.org/contact_us?id=0001

Reasons for Concern
A brief pamphlet on early signs of potential concern for children not yet in school. California Department of Education. (2010) *"Reasons for Concern That Your Child or a Child in Your Care May Need Special Help."* Sacramento. www.dds.ca.gov/EarlyStart/docs/ReasonsForConcern_English.pdf.

Special Needs Organizations and Information

ADDers.org
This organization promotes awareness of Attention Deficit/Hyperactivity Disorder and provides information and practical help to sufferers, both adults and children, and their families in the UK and around the world. www.ADDers.org

ADHD Owner's Manual
www.edutechsbs.com/adhd

American Council of the Blind (ACB)
The American Council of the Blind strives to increase the independence, security, equality of opportunity, and quality of life, for all blind and visually-impaired people.

> American Council of the Blind
> 1703 N. Beauregard St., Suite 420
> Alexandria, VA 22311
> Local: (202) 467-5081
> Toll Free: (800) 424-8666
> Fax: (703) 465-5085
> Email: info@acb.org
> Website: www.acb.org

American Diabetes Association (ADA)
The ADA's mission is to prevent and cure diabetes and to improve the lives of all people affected by diabetes.

> American Diabetes Association
> 2451 Crystal Drive, Suite 900
> Arlington, VA 22202
> Toll Free: 1-800-DIABETES (800-342-2383)
> Website: www.diabetes.org

American Foundation for the Blind (AFB)

The American Foundation for the Blind (AFB) removes barriers, creates solutions, and expands possibilities so people with vision loss can achieve their full potential.

> American Foundation for the Blind
> 2 Penn Plaza, Suite 1102
> New York, NY 10121
> Local: (212) 502-7600
> Fax: (888) 545-8331
> Website: www.afb.org

American Society for Deaf Children (ASDC)

ASDC is the premier source of information for people who must make decisions about deaf children: providers, educators, legislators, and advocates.

American Printing House for the Blind, Inc.

> 1839 Frankfort Avenue, Louisville, KY 40206
> Toll Free: (800) 223-1839, ext. 705
> Email: resource@aph.org
> Website: louis.aph.org/catalog/CategoryInfo.aspx?cid=152

American Society for Deaf Children

> 800 Florida Avenue, NE #2047
> Washington, DC 20002-3695
> Toll Free: (800) 942-2732 (ASDC)
> Fax: (410) 795-0965
> Website: www.deafchildren.org

National Attention Deficit Disorder Association (ADDA)

The Attention Deficit Disorder Association (ADDA) has become the source for information and resources exclusively for and about adult ADHD. ADDA brings together scientific perspectives and the human experience to generate hope, awareness, empowerment and connections worldwide in the field of ADHD.

Attention Deficit Disorder Association

    Toll Free: (800) 939-1019

    Email Form: https://add.org/contact-adda

    Website: www.add.org

Autism Society of America

The Autism Society, the nation's leading grassroots autism organization, exists to improve the lives of all affected by autism. They do this by increasing public awareness about the day-to-day issues faced by people on the spectrum, advocating for appropriate services for individuals across the lifespan, and providing the latest information regarding treatment, education, research and advocacy.

    Autism Society of America

    4340 East-West Hwy, Suite 350

    Bethesda, Maryland 20814

    Local: (301) 657-0881

    Toll Free: (800) 3AUTISM (800) 328-8476

    Email: info@autism-society.org

    Website: www.autism-society.org

Brain Injury Association of America (BIAA)

The Brain Injury Association of America (BIAA) is the country's oldest and largest nationwide brain injury advocacy organization. Their mission is to advance awareness, research, treatment and education and to improve the quality of life for all individuals impacted by brain injury.

    Brain Injury Association of America

    1608 Spring Hill Road, Suite 110

    Vienna, VA 22182

    Local: (703) 761-0750

    Fax: (703) 761-0755

    Website: www.biausa.org

Can Do!

Can Do! was founded, created and launched in October 1997 by ability awareness educator and school counselor, Maribeth Bush. Since then, through ever-growing grassroots support, Can Do! has reached and inspired children, teens, and adults in over 16 countries around the world. www.ucando.org

Children's Assistance Center (ECAC)

Parent Training and Info Center: The Exceptional Children's Assistance Center is a private non-profit organization that helps parents navigate the special education maze and provides them with the information and tools to be an informed and active participant in their child's education.

Exceptional Children's Assistance Center

907 Barra Row, Suites 102/103
Davidson, NC 28036
Local: (704) 892-1321
Fax: (704) 892-5028
Parent Info Line: (800) 962-6817
Email: ecac@ecacmail.org
Website: www.ecac-parentcenter.org

The Cooke Center

The Cooke Center is a non-sectarian, non-profit private provider of special education services in New York City, offering a school for students ages 5-21, as well as consulting and training services.

Cooke Center for Learning and Development
475 Riverside Drive, Suite 730
New York, NY 10115
Local: 212-280-4473
Email: info@cookecenter.org
Website: www.cookecenter.org

Down Syndrome: For New Parents

A resource for new parents, friends and family to share the joy, love, hardships, and fun of raising a child with Down syndrome. www.downsyn.com/joomla

The National Down Syndrome Congress (NDSC)

The National Down Syndrome Congress (NDSC) is a membership-sustained not-for-profit organization dedicated to an improved world for individuals with Down syndrome. Founded in 1973, they are considered the leading national resource of support and information for anyone touched by or seeking to learn about Down syndrome, from the moment of a prenatal diagnosis through adulthood.

>30 Mandell Court, Suite 108
>Roswell, GA 30076
>Toll Free: (800) 232-6372
>Local: (770) 604-9500
>Fax: (770) 604-9898
>Email: info@ndsccenter.org
>Website: www.ndsccenter.org

The National Down Syndrome Society

The leading human rights organization for all people with Down syndrome. They envision a world in which all people with Down syndrome have the opportunity to enhance their quality of life, realize their life aspirations and become valued members of welcoming communities.

>The National Down Syndrome Society
>8 E 41st Street, 8th Floor
>New York, New York, 10017
>Toll Free: (800) 221-4602
>Email: info@ndss.org
>Website: www.ndss.org

Growth Charts for Children with Down Syndrome

www.growthcharts.com

IN*Source - Special Education Parent Support

Provides Indiana families and service providers the information and training necessary to assure effective educational programs and appropriate services for children and young adults with disabilities.

>Indiana Resource Center for Families with Special Needs
>1703 South Ironwood Drive
>South Bend, Indiana 46613
>Local: (574) 234-7101
>Toll Free: (800) 332-4433
>Fax: (574) 234-7279
>Email: insource@insource.org
>Website: www.insource.org

Kenneth Jernigan: 'power to the blind'

Raffensperger, Gene. (1974) "Kenneth Jernigan: 'power to the blind.'" The Des Moines Sunday Register. Retrieved from: http://www.braillerman.com/jernigan.htm

Louis Database

The American Printing House for the Blind (APH) maintains and promotes the Louis Database of Accessible Materials, named in honor of Louis Braille. Louis contains information on accessible print materials produced by about 160 organizations throughout the United States. These materials include books in braille, large print, audio, and electronic file format.

National Center for Learning Disabilities (NCLD)

The mission of NCLD is to improve the lives of the 1 in 5 children and adults nationwide with learning and attention issues by empowering parents and young adults, transforming schools and advocating for equal rights and opportunities.

> National Center for Learning Disabilities
> 32 Laight Street, Second Floor
> New York, NY 10013
> Website: www.ncld.org

Parent Educational Advocacy Training Center (PEATC)

> PEATC builds positive futures for Virginia's children by working collaboratively with families, schools and communities in order to improve opportunities for excellence in education and success in school and community life.
> Parent Educational Advocacy Training Center
> 8003 Forbes Place
> Suite 310
> Springfield, VA 22151
> Local: (703) 923-0010
> Toll Free: (800) 869-6782
> Email: partners@peatc.org
> Website: www.peatc.org

Parents Helping Parents

A parent-directed agency that provides support, training and information to individuals with any special need and their families. www.php.com

Teaching the ADD Child

Great ideas for educators and parents. www.lessontutor.com/addgen-home.html

Narrative Television Network (NTN)

Since 1988, NTN has been a leader in making television, movies, and educational programming accessible to the nation's 13 million people who are blind and visually impaired and their families.

> Narrative Television Network
> 5840 South Memorial Drive, Suite 312
> Tulsa, Oklahoma 74145-9082
> Toll Free: 800-801-8184
> Local: (918) 627-1000
> Fax (918) 627-4101
> Email: info@narrativetv.com
> Website: www.narrativetv.com

Vision of Children Foundation (VOC)

The mission of the Vision of Children Foundation is to cure hereditary childhood blindness and other vision disorders and to improve the lives of visually impaired individuals and their families.

> The Vision of Children Foundation
> 12555 High Bluff Drive, Suite 330
> San Diego, CA 92130
> Local: 858.314.7917
> Fax: 858.314.7920
> Email: info@visionofchildren.org
> Website: www.visionofchildren.org

If you enjoyed reading Finding Einstein: My IEP Journey, please go to Amazon and leave a review. For self-published authors like me, getting reviews (especially on Amazon) means I can submit my books for advertising. Reviews also help you share your reading experience with new readers. So please leave a review. It's a win-win for everyone!

Notes

Notes

Notes

About the Author

Lia Martin (aka Lia P) is a wife, mother, advocate and writer who has worked as an administrative professional, sitcom writer and television executive with deals at ABC and HBO Independent Productions. She is also co-host of the new parenting podcast, "Grab a Bottle." She is raising two children and has volunteered in leadership roles with child-centered organizations since high school. She is the daughter of award winning author, J Everett Prewitt. She resides in California with her husband, daughter and twice exceptional son. Finding Einstein: My IEP Journey is her first book.

Please visit: www.myiepjourney.com for more information and inspiration.